A Tale of True Love

A True Story

by

Afia Khatun

A Tale of True Love

Formatted by Enterprise Book Services, LLC

BISMILLAH

HIR- RAHMAN NIR RAHEEM

In the name of Allah, the Most Gracious, the Most Merciful

Acknowledgements

To my husband Ali, thank you for being a part of our journey, for believing in us, for being there no matter what & never letting me down- Congratulations on 10 amazing years of marriage and many more to come inshallah, here's to the next chapter in our lives.

To Nazreen Altaf, the selfless solicitor who went above & beyond her legal capacity to desperately bring a husband and wife together. Nazreen your presence was truly a blessing, you believed in & fought for us and we will never forget that. I pray that God grants you and your family good health & every happiness in life.

To Debbie, thank you for being there, for caring for me like a mother should, for involving yourself when no one else would, for those acts of kindness you so humbly took on. This I cannot forget, know that you are now a part of this beautiful journey.

For Ali's family in Afghanistan, my in-laws.

The people who without undue hesitation welcomed a stranger into their lives, their home, their culture. Who never turned their back on me or disapproved when it was too easy to do so. Those who sent a message to others & put their son's happiness before their Pride or Culture. Who showered me with so much affection that I forgot my pain, who cared for me better than their own that I became their own.

You are truly the hero's here & I love you so much for it.

Glossary

Desi- A loose term for the people, cultures, and products of the Indian subcontinent or South Asia.

Haji- A Muslim male who has visited Makkah & performed pilgrimage- one of the five pillars of Islam.

Freshi – A person who just arrived 'stepped off the boat/lorry/plane' from their native country, struggles to speak the local language, has limited sense of current fashion or style.

Boroaffa- Big sister -in a respectful manner.

Lal Affa- Red Sister.

Abba- Dad

Deen- Faith

Jaan- Life- Is widely used as a term in East Asian countries to address your spouse.

Izzat- Pride/honour

Nikah- Muslim marriage ceremony

Imam- An Islamic leadership position usually the worship leader of a mosque.

Alhamdulillah- All praise be to Allah/thanks god

Lengha- An Indian outfit made up of a skirt and top

Shalwar Kameez- Traditional Indian/Asian dress

Inshallah- God willing

Sunnat- An act completed by the Prophet Mohammed (PBUH- Peace be upon him)

Halal- An Arabic word for permissible, in terms of food its food that is permissible according to Islamic law.

Qubool Hai- I accept.

Kuchi- Traditional Afghan dress

Mashallah- Expresses appreciation, joy, praise to God for an event or person mentioned

Henna- A dye prepared from a plant used as a form of body art.

Quran- The holy book in Islam

Dua- A prayer to God

Allah- Arabic word for God used by Muslims

The Meeting

I am a British born Bengali girl bought up in a standard desi household shared by my mum, dad and six siblings.

We have quite a typical set up of a large family and dad being a Restaurateur/property developer/mosque chairman and generally a local community man not to mention a Haji. Mum is a house wife and as you would expect we had quite a strict Bengali upbringing. It went somewhat like this; school, home, pray, eat, attend mosque, a little TV then back to bed and do it all over again. Going out with friends, having a mobile phone, going on school trips were all things that were usually out of the question and would require lengthy mediation before my parents would even consider. This is where my story begins......

It was the 12th June 2006, I was 16 years old and taking my GCSE exams at my local Upper School. I didn't particularly know what I wanted to do after school, I had no real plans or direction that I wanted to head in, instead I would just take each day as it came. It was a beautiful summers day and I needed to get out so I told my parents that I had an exam to sit that day at school. In fact, I lied as an excuse to get out of the house and hang out with my friends. As my school was next to a park, now and again I would skive off by making my way to school then diverting to the park. I'd use the excuse of an exam/extra tuitions and sit in the park most of the day with my friends as I knew it would be difficult to do so otherwise.

I was in the park with two friends, Shuz and Shaz, one of them lived in a small council house nearby with several of her siblings, nieces and nephews etc although I don't quite know how they all squeezed in there and the other Shaz was a somewhat a troubled girl. Shaz's parents had both passed away and she was living with different foster families after being turfed out of her Uncles place not long ago. Whilst she was quite the rebel she was the kind of girl that would follow the crowd and was easily led, I felt sympathy for her, in the world without her parents and felt part of her behaviour was her craving attention. Shuz's younger sister Rash was a slim, kind natured girl who used to tag along with us at times although she was a few years younger.

We sat in the park bored one afternoon, listening to music on our phones and chatting amongst ourselves when we saw this geeky looking boy walking towards us. I say boy because of the way he was dressed but as he came closer he was clearly old enough to be a man. We must have been extremely bored as we made our way over to him, albeit I have no idea what for. He certainly didn't have the looks and seemed very shy and reserved, Shuz and Shaz would smoke and I was partial to a passive drag now and again, although I couldn't stand the smell. We asked him for a fag, that's when we learnt that he couldn't speak English, Shuz could speak good Urdu that she had picked up from films, well good meaning better than any of us, so she understood some of his response. He didn't have any fags, so we asked him if he had any money, again I don't know what we were planning.

He smiled, 'Yes,' he said nodding his head.

We looked at each other with thoughts in our head until he surprised us and pulled out some coppers from his pockets. We all cracked up with laughter and told him to get lost, we didn't know his name but he told us he was getting his wages later that day. We told him to meet us in the same place in a few hours after he had been paid. I guess he thought he would get the benefit of our company, whilst we had other ideas of how to spend his money. We hung around in the park for the time being and a few hours later he came back with a big grin on his face. He emptied his pockets a second time and even more coins came spilling out, we couldn't control our laughter and ended up in tears. He gave us all a handshake as a greeting as we carried on dying of laughter and that's how he was named 'handshake boy'.

The next day we were all in the park again sitting on the swings. I was wearing a turquoise colour Asian style dress that my uncle had made for me, I wore it with some jeans to westernise it, a thin nude colour hoodie and I had my hair down with a hijab thrown over. At the time I had quite an East meets West, eclectic style and liked to add my own twist to an outfit. These two young guys came over, I knew they were coming over with a motive so for a laugh I faked that I was a 'freshi' and couldn't speak English. They started chatting to Shuz and Shaz asking about me and why I wasn't talking. To give you some context Shuz & Shaz were not exactly the best catch hence why they didn't necessarily get any immediate attention. I told them my name was Ayesha which wasn't exactly the truth. I knew they were after my phone number and after a while they realised that I wasn't a Freshi. One of them was skinny and spotty, the sort you wouldn't really give a second look but the other guy he was alright. They introduced themselves, the skinny guy was Nasim and the other was 'Ali'. I didn't know where they were from and didn't really ask to be honest, which was unusual for me. Ali gave me his number and asked me to ring him so he could save mine. I didn't know what to do as I had only just met the guy but we were so bored so I changed my phone to private number and rang him although I have no idea why I did that.

He just looked at me in a way that is un describable and said, 'I don't need a private number, if you're not going to give me your number then don't bother'.

No guy had ever spoken to me like that before, I was annoyed but at the same time there was something I liked about him. He was 5'6, fair skinned, healthy thick black hair, gelled back or even oiled, who knows. I didn't take much notice of what he was wearing but he smelt good, had small brown eyes, bright white teeth and sported these distinct blue and white Adidas trainers. I ended up giving him my number, we didn't really say much at the time just the usual small talk and he was on his way with his friend.

A little while after he left he rang me, we started chatting generally, asking questions. I wasn't in the mood to chat so I made excuses and kept hanging up on him but he was persistent and kept ringing back. I could see him sitting a fair bit away from us in the park on the grass, me Shuz and Shaz grew concerned.

Shuz looked at me and questioned, 'Why did you give him your number? He won't leave you alone now, he might give it out to his friends or stalk you.'

I panicked and so we marched over to Ali and his mate, we told him to stop ringing me. He just laughed at us, so I got one of Shuz's male friends to ring me and act like he was my cousin to scare them and get them to back off. They didn't take much notice and carried on, after arguing with them for a while we just walked away. It was almost 3:30pm, I knew I had to walk back to school and pose waiting to be picked up so I began to pace down the park back to school.

At home Ali kept ringing me, I continued to decline his call but I soon came to realise that he was not a quitter. He would ring at all times of the day, I thought it would die down and he would get bored. I only gave him my number in the heat of the moment out of boredom. Eventually I got fed up of hanging up and trying to ignore him so this is when we started properly chatting. I was not actually allowed a phone, the one I did have was an 'undercover' Nokia brick as they call them now. Me and my eldest sister, Boroaffa shared a room and we both had under cover phones, so there were no surprises. Whilst me and Ali began chatting, I almost forgot that I gave him a false name of Ayesha but managed to keep the pretence up for a bit. I didn't know where this was going to go and the first time I had spoken to a guy outside of my community, hence the name to protect me in case it went wrong. Although it wasn't a complete lie as its common in the Asian/Bengali community to have more than one name, a home name & a proper registered name. The home name is usually something freshi and embarrassing but Ayesha was the name my grandmother in Bangladesh gave me and called me by. We chatted generally, what do you do? How old are you? Where are you from? He was 18 and I had just turned 16, I made up so many lies about myself that I was finding it difficult to remember the lies from the truth but I was just testing the water first I thought. I told Ali that my older sister was married with a taxi driver husband living in Birmingham, although she was unmarried still living at home. He believed me but kept asking me things about it and continued to question me. He persistently asked me where I lived, yeah right, I thought like I was going to tell him that. He was attending Northampton College and working evenings at a takeaway called Hot 4 you, I know right the shop name is so cheesy & ironic. We began to spend more time talking to each other on the phone although nothing too serious. I would continue to sneak out and meet him mostly in the park as neither of us could drive and it was the closest place away from prying eyes. Sometimes I would meet him with Shuz and Shaz but most of the time alone as I trusted him now and felt comfortable alone although I still didn't know loads about him. It felt strange in many ways but good at the same time, I acted different with him than I would usually. I knew there was something about him I liked, but I continued to play hard to get as if I wasn't bothered, we were still just friends at that point and I was happy with that.

Ali came cycling through the park on his bike one day, he saw us and stopped to talk. He had just come from his last exam at college, as he came towards us I could feel myself getting hot and bothered. Somehow the conversation turned deep and everyone started questioning him, where he was from and what religion he was although we had a good idea already. He was a Muslim, from Italy, that would explain him wearing the blue Italian T-shirt all the time I thought. He did have a slight Italian look to him but his accent just didn't make sense. He was showing us pictures on his phone then out of nowhere he pulls out a picture of a girl named Sarah. He said she was his girlfriend, a Turkish girl who attended the same upper school as us. I was so angry, I couldn't believe it, why hadn't he mentioned it before? Why did he want my number in the first place?

But then I only gave him my number for a laugh I thought, to pass time so why should I care? I just turned away as though I wasn't interested. I was fuming inside but I just gave it my usual hard girl act and didn't let on.

After a few days, coincidentally I saw her in school, the girl from the picture, Sara. I examined her from afar at first, a short, slim girl, bare faced with curly mid length light hair and no distinguishing features, she didn't look his type I thought although I was certainly no expert of 'his type' just yet. I approached her whilst she was stood with her group of friends and began to question her about Ali, I wasn't looking for trouble, just intrigued so I asked if she knew him and how they met. She was confused and understandably wanted to know why I was asking these questions, she began to annoy me so it ended with me shouting at her and walking away. She wasn't exactly pretty and she was so shy and timid, I could've taken her like that I thought but she didn't look like a fighter so I didn't bother. Although I found out about her I was still speaking to Ali on the phone, I don't know why, I suppose because we were just friends and neither of us had yet declared anything more than this to each other. After a few weeks Ali told me Sara ended it with him, he immediately suspected my involvement which I denied but he didn't seem too bothered about it to be honest. Maybe she got put off by me or maybe she just went off him, who knows.

I continued to meet Ali now and then although one afternoon I genuinely had an exam so I was in school but Ali came to see me with his mates in the park, he told Shuz to ring me to come to the park when I'd finished. After I came out of the exam hall I saw 14 missed calls from Shuz. I called her back frantically thinking the worst, she explained Ali was here to see me, he demanded that they call me, he wouldn't leave without seeing me.

I was puzzled as I made my way over to the park, 'What's wrong?' I asked him.

'Nothing', he said, he just acted normal as though he didn't care, he said hi and chatted.

I was annoyed why did he seem so desperate to see me not long ago and now he just wasn't bothered. As he was leaving he gave everyone a handshake except me, he turned around to walk off. After meeting handshake boy that was our greeting, when we would see each other as oppose to a boy & girl hugging which the idea of would just be uncomfortable, instead we would greet and leave with a handshake. After rushing to the park, he was just playing with me, I was beyond annoyed, as he walked away he turned back and grinned at me followed by a wink. What the hell was that I thought, crazy guy. Him and his mates were sitting in the park, I started to walk back to school as it was almost 3:30pm. As I began walking I got a text from Ali, it read 'you look beautiful when your angry'. I looked around at him and tried to smile sarcastically, I was still annoyed but couldn't hide my blushing face.

As time went on we chatted regularly, it was now close to 6 months that we had met. We could chat for hours on end, I found myself not wanting to hang up, feeling sad when it was time say goodbye and would often go to bed thinking about what we had discussed. He would ring me after he finished at the takeaway as he was walking home, by this time we knew we had feelings for one another but we were just taking it slow or so I thought. Having received my GCSE results, I decided to stick with Shuz and Shaz and started a NVQ in Business Admin at a local Training Centre. I knew I could do better but part of me wanted to stay with them and the other option was Sixth form which I couldn't bear the thought of, the idea of being cooped up in that school for another 2 years didn't appeal to me. One night, we chatted from 12am till 5am knowing that we both had to be up for 8am that morning, but we didn't seem too bothered. It was at that point I knew we had strong feelings for each other otherwise why would I talk to a guy for that long and put myself through that?

Ali rang me one night as normal, told me he had something to tell me

'Ok, go for it' I replied.

'I love you' he said.

I froze I didn't know what to say, I had very strong feelings for him but didn't feel as though I could say I loved him just yet. I knew the automatic response should be me reiterating my feelings of love back to him but I didn't want to be fake.

So, I replied 'thank you', I felt terrible about it but knew I did the right thing, he was just quiet but he told me he understood that it would take time.

By now we would usually meet up in a different park now, Abington Park which was closer to my house. I know it's very cliché going from one park to the next but it was convenient and we were less likely to be seen together not to mention neither of us could still drive yet so it was difficult to go anywhere too far. Come rain, shine or snow nothing would come in our way, we would always make the effort to meet 2-3 times a week.

Soon after I gave him those words he was longing for, I felt it, so I said it, I declared my love for him. I could tell he was ecstatic, that day I went to meet him and bought him a gift, a picture frame with a photo of us in it. I guess he felt it was to symbolise my commitment, I was a serious girlfriend and he could proudly put this picture up. It meant so much to him and he loved it, it was just a plain boring frame with a picture of us I printed off my phone but he couldn't stop smiling. By this time, I had told him everything about me, my real name and about my family. He even guessed where I lived which turned out to be only a few streets away from him. I gave him the first two letters of my street name and he guessed by looking it up on the big map they had on the wall of the takeaway.

There was a coffee shop in Abington Park and I'm sure we were their best customers as we were there literally every day. It was family run and a lot of the time the youngest son about twenty years old or so used to serve us and give us a cheeky smile every time as if he knew something we didn't. In a way the café staff watched our relationship blossom and became part of our story. We were their regulars and they got to know our 'usual' hot drink orders. As our relationship grew it became more and more difficult to try to make excuses to get out of the house to meet, I'm not sure why the sudden change but there were more questions and hurdles to overcome. Then one day I came home from the Training Centre as normal, as I entered the house I had this strange feeling, call it an intuition, I could just feel that something bad was going to happen and that it was going to begin from a phone call.

Let's get ready to get rumbled

That evening I was upstairs in my room getting changed when my mum came barging in, she looked at me in a way I can only describe as both mad and disappointed at the same time.

'Somebody's just phoned the house asking to speak to your dad' she shouted.

'Yeah so what' I replied calmly although truthfully petrified.

'I told them he wasn't in so they told me instead, they told me that you have been meeting an Afghani boy for some time now!'. She was furious, 'Is this true she demanded?'

I was in total shock, that was it, it's all over now, everyone will find out everything. So, I backtracked for a minute, mum had already found my undercover phone not long ago at which time I managed to convince her it was a friend's and that I would be returning it to her. Whatever was going to come out of my mouth had to be damn good or I was done for. I knew that over the last few weeks Shuz & Rash had genuinely been getting calls to their house from random guys saying the same thing, that they had been up to no good. However, mine was true and I knew it so I told mum about the same calls my friends had been getting and that there was nothing to worry about, just jealous people trying to cause trouble. In the back of my mind I knew that if I wasn't involved in anything like this then no one would have any reason to do this either truthfully or as a prank.

When dad came home he got one of the phone calls too, I was horrified he was going to hit the roof so I told him the same thing, I don't know if they bought it at first but then I gave Shuz's dads name and their home telephone number to check with him and back up my story. This made it more feasible and they would be able to corroborate my version of events. I knew mum and dad wouldn't back down easily, even Boroaffa was looking at me with a face like thunder, with an expression of good luck your screwed. Then came the questions, why don't you ever have a fixed finishing time at the training centre? Why do you get the bus every day? There was clearly a need to probe me now, I used to tell them I didn't have a fixed finishing time so I could meet Ali after my lessons as this was the best way to ensure I'd be able to meet him regularly. By this time, me and Ali were serious about each other, well as serious as a mature 16 & 18 year old could get and I knew he wasn't just someone I could forget about. I started to panic when they were asking me all these questions, surely they would catch me out somewhere, it was a Thursday evening and dad said he would drop me and pick me up to the training centre from now on. My heart sank, I knew that this is how it would always be and that it would be almost impossible to make excuses to meet Ali again.

That night my stomach was churning, I felt sick thinking about it all, I didn't know what to do. I rang Ali, he was at the takeaway working, I told him everything. Although we were serious about each other part of me wondered whether he'd care, it was fun while it lasted but maybe it was just getting complicated, he is a young guy after all, right? I told him that we would have to cool it down for a while, I was even struggling to find a chance to call him about that, it was a bit of a mess and I was still a bit confused.

The next morning dad took me to the training centre as promised, I could tell he was annoyed with a stern look on his face. I love my dad and I am certainly a daddy's girl so I felt embarrassed and upset that I put him in that position. He would have to wake up early every morning after working late at the restaurant just because I couldn't be trusted. When we arrived, he parked up and came in with me, he approached the manager of the centre. 'Has my daughter been attending all her classes at the centre?' he asked.

I stood back with my head down in shame. 'Yes of course, she is one of our top students' she replied.

I was relieved although not for long, he then went on to ask this geeky Bengali girl that worked there the same question. Oh no I thought, I didn't really speak to her and she seemed quite the nosey type, this wasn't going to end well. Dad proceeded to ask her whether I have fixed start and finish times, I gave her that Bengali sisterhood 'cover for me' look. As a freshi she ignored my obvious signal to her and told dad the truth that my times were fixed 9-4. My dad turned to me in disappointment, I was annoyed at her but felt worse about dad's disappointment.

At 4pm the same day mum and Boroaffa came to pick me up, dad was at work and Boroaffa could drive, there was an awkward silence in the car the whole way back. When we got home Boroaffa told me how stupid I was getting caught with this kind of thing and that mum and dad would always be watching now. The next day was Saturday by this time I was anxious to see Ali, I didn't know how it was going to affect our relationship, I just knew that if we couldn't meet up then basically there was no relationship. Talking on the phone is all well and good but meeting face to face was different, maybe it was a test of our relationship, I was so confused.

That night I crept into the spare room and rang Ali, I told him that we had to leave, we had to run away to be together or it was never going to work. My parents would keep such a close eye on me that I would never be able to meet him, I just couldn't take the risk of losing him because of this. He was busy at work as it was a Saturday night, I broke down whilst telling him what I thought we had to do, I slightly mislead him and gave him the impression there was potential I could be shipped off back home to get married, he was shocked. He'd heard about these things but didn't think it still happened, I paused maybe he would say it's not my problem, I couldn't gage his reaction at first.

By this time Ali had already told me a while back that he wasn't a British citizen and that he was here as a student from Afghanistan. He was so worried when he told me and to be honest I didn't really know what it meant so I was like yeah, whatever that's fine.

As I sobbed he reassured me, 'Calm down' he said 'What you are saying is a very big decision, are you absolutely sure this is what you want?'

'Yes, I'm sure' I replied, 'I've been thinking about it a lot and this is what we have to do to be together'.

I wanted to leave the next day, Sunday but Ali said no, we should wait until the Monday to make it look as normal as possible. I didn't care I just wanted to get out and fall into Ali's arms where I felt somewhat at ease. That night he told me to pack my things, bearing in mind girls have hundreds of 'essentials' I managed to narrow it down. It was a strange feeling, I was packing not to go on holiday, I didn't know where we were going or if or when we'd be back. We had silly conversations about what to take, Ali was going to pack a travel iron & me my straighteners, looking back it reflects a rare glimpse of our immaturity at that age as generally we were both quite mature.

Ali came up with a plan, the only way I could take my things with me was in hiding and I was already being watched like a hawk at home. I put my things into a Northampton College drawstring bag, it was something I got at the open day at the college.

I was wading through all sorts of stuff to decide what to take with me, I even went up to get some extra bits I had in the attic cupboards, my brothers were young and didn't understand much but the eldest Abdullah whom we addressed as Abs asked me,

' Lal affa, what are you looking for? Shall I help you?'

'No, it's ok', I replied, 'Don't look it's something for you' I lied.

Affa means sister and Lal means red in Bengali, I don't know how I got that name but that's what my younger siblings and cousins would call me to differentiate as otherwise everyone would be called Affa. In our culture as a form of respect to your elder sisters/brothers you don't call them by name, rather as sister or brother.

We have a small front garden where big wheelie bins are kept, I opened the front door and in order not to raise suspicion I took the bin bags out with me alongside the college bag full of stuff. I threw the bin bags in the bins and hid the college bag in the corner of the front garden next to the wall, I hesitated a moment. What if dad finishes work late from the restaurant and if he saw this at a glance it would all be over, so I swung it over the neighbour's front garden instead and hid it in the corner. It was still risky but I knew it was late so they wouldn't come out to see it, besides Ali would finish work at 12 am and the plan was he would walk past my house as it was his normal route home, swing his arm into next doors front garden and grab the bag carrying it on his back which is exactly what he did that night.

The next day was Sunday 17th December 2008, it was 24 hours before I was planning to run away from home. I was terrified and excited at the same time, whilst I felt like I had little choice it took a lot of courage to make that decision for a girl who hadn't even walked to the corner shop on her own. I hadn't told anybody about what I was going to do, not even

Boroaffa, although I trusted her I couldn't take the risk of her stopping me. She already knew that me and Ali were together but no idea of what was about to take place.

The Runaway

Monday 18th December 2008, I got up from bed as normal and was getting ready to go to my 'Training Course'. I rang Ali as I got changed to make sure he was up, I don't think he even slept that night thinking of the day to come. I can't say I could blame him as naturally he would get all the grief because he was the guy. Dad would drop me and my sisters off together, them to school and me to the training centre, so we all crammed into the car. Dad drove a Benz-C Class, although not a huge car man you could tell it was his pride and joy but why not for a man who worked hard day and night to provide for his family. He drove up to a park next to the Training centre and told me to walk the rest of the way so he didn't have to turn the car around to drop my sisters to school in the opposite direction. As I stepped out of the car, I couldn't help but glance back and take one last look at my family. I didn't know if or when I would ever see them again or under what circumstances and believe me that was tough. As much as I love Ali and didn't regret what I was doing it was a moment of reflection, I was essentially leaving behind my family of 16 years but I felt I had little choice.

My eyes began to water and I quickly walked on, dad called out behind me 'be careful crossing the road sweetheart', in his own Bengali way of course.

I became riled with guilt, one person whom I felt hardest to leave was dad, my Abba. Everyone says the same thing, right? My dad's great, he's the best, but I guarantee you one thing, my dad is the kindest, most generous, honest person you would ever meet. He is a well-known figure in the local community, restaurateur, Chef by trade, man of deen & religion, the local mosque chairman & treasurer, trusted by many but most of all loved by all. Not one person could say a bad word about him, no grudges, no enemies, dad has his faith at the forefront of anything he does which teaches us to be kind to others, be truthful, respectful and fulfil all your duties. Whenever anyone would ask about my dad a huge smile would come over them when I would repeat his name. He built his reputation himself, it wasn't handed to him on a plate nor was he boastful, this is the character of a man I'm proud to call my father.

All us sisters are daddy's girls, if I ever wanted to go somewhere I would ask dad, I wouldn't risk it with mum. She would interrogate me with questions and then just say no anyway but dad listened and asked questions he needed to whilst considering what was being asked. We lived in a bit of a nest, even the local school fayre was off limits by mum but one year we sneaked out anyway. When dad heard he came to meet us there and supposedly give us a telling off from mum but instead he tracked us down and gave us extra spending money and told us not to be late coming home.

I waited a few minutes after getting out the car then walked to the nearby park we passed as this is where I agreed to meet Ali. I think at this point our lives revolved around parks right?, I sat on the bench in the cold, thoughts were running through my head. What if he changed his mind or didn't love me enough? Was I doing the right thing? Would my family understand? I was anxious, if he didn't come then apart from it being highly embarrassing, it would break my heart. This was a girl who would struggle to sneak to the corner shop or local fayre and here I was attempting something as big as this. As I sat and pondered I saw him coming towards me with a huge gym bag on his shoulder. He gave me a hug as he approached and whispered, 'last chance, are you sure you want to do this?' I resoundingly answered,

'Yes Jaan I'm sure'. We went to the Lloyds TSB branch in town where Ali withdrew all that was in his account, all of about £800 and he had another £250 in his pocket that he borrowed from his brother although he hadn't told him the purpose of the loan. As we walked through town to the train station, it felt strange, we both felt like we didn't really have to worry about being careful, although we hadn't quite escaped yet, even so this new confidence had kicked in and I didn't care if anyone saw us. On the way we saw one of Ali's classmates from College, they stopped and exchanged words for a few minutes but of course he didn't let on where he was going. Ali stood in the train station ticket queue, I didn't have a clue where we were going but we had talked about going to Scotland to get married in Gretna Green as I was 16. Completely mad, but it gave us hope in a way I guess, we both switched our phones off as I knew once word got out our phones would be going off like mad to track us down.

The train journey to Edinburgh felt like forever, when we finally arrived 6 hours later we didn't have a clue where we were. I had never been to the seaside let alone another country or so far away from home. We picked up some maps and started to look for the closest hotel as we were both exhausted and needed to rest. We walked up steep streets and arrived at a revolving door of a hotel lobby, as we walked in my bag got stuck in the doors and Ali stared and laughed at me whilst I managed to pull myself free. I felt as if I was in another world, everywhere we went the hotels were either full or too expensive. We ended up staying in a premier inn for £50 a night just to get our heads down for the day that was about to come.

The next morning, I switched my phone on to check and saw too many missed calls and texts to count, the guilt well and truly set in but it was done now. We decided to look for some youth help or hostel type accommodation, someone to help us or the equivalent of what was known as connexions back in Northampton which was an organisation that helped young people in all sorts of situations. We weren't having much luck, we walked for hours up steep streets trying to follow maps but we were making no real progress.

Eventually we approached a local police station, I knew my family would be worried sick and I needed to let them know I was ok no matter what. For all they knew I was abducted or worse and I knew it wasn't fair. I felt sick walking into the station like a criminal, wondering if it was the right thing to do but Ali reassured me it was. I explained the situation to the lady on the front desk and she took me into a room and sat me down. She asked me numerous questions, I told her to give my family a message, tell them I was ok, not to worry and that I didn't want to come home. Ali sat with me while I told her what happened in more detail. I could tell by her expression that she had suspicions that Ali was forcing me to do this but I didn't care as I knew that was not the case. Afterwards we asked her if she knew anywhere relatively cheap that we could stay the night. She ordered us a taxi and within 20 minutes we arrived at a youth hostel. It looked decent, well for £20 a night we couldn't complain, there was one of those boxes in our room where you put £1 in to watch TV for an hour. We sat on the bed with EastEnders on, we both stared at the screen looking right through the TV thinking about what we had done. We didn't tell anyone we were going to do this, what was everyone thinking? Part of me couldn't believe I had done this and part of me was terrified. What about my family I thought. What would they do when they found out? Had I done the right thing? What were my brothers and sisters going to think?

That night we talked realistically about what our plans where, we knew coming to Scotland was a silly idea and we could never make a life here. We could barely understand the accent, this wasn't our area and neither of us liked it so far away from home, we decided to go a bit closer to home, at least in the same region anyway. I don't know why but we decided on Leicester to start a new life. We closed our eyes for a blink of sleep and got up at 5am for a long train journey back. When we arrived in Leicester I felt a bit better, we were not in completely alien surroundings anymore although you could argue we were. I had never been to this part of Leicester before, the English part. I was so used to the Asian part, going to Belgrave centre every year for family Eid shopping, we would even park on the same road every time, Buller Road. We were tired from the journey so we found the nearest Holiday Inn, dumped our belongings and went to have something to eat at a local takeaway. By this time, we had already spent at least £200 of the cash we had as the cost of the train tickets and hotels was adding up. The room we got at Holiday Inn was nice and cosy, Ali fell asleep after a while and I watched him wondering what tomorrow would bring.

The next day we left the hotel and began looking in shop windows for a room to rent as we knew we couldn't stay in hotels for much longer. All day we must have rang at least thirty different rooms and it wasn't looking good. Luckily with some patience we finally found one, the landlords name was Jee and he also lived in the house. He was kind and we were lucky as he got the room ready for us the same day, we waited in KFC for his call to let us know the room was ready. When we got there, we inspected the room although we had no other choice but it was fine and we both sighed with some relief. For the next few weeks we tried to lead a normal life, Ali was looking for a job and I thought about starting at a nearby college. I think in some silly way I thought we could make it work here but times were tough. Every penny we spent on rent, food and clothes was money we didn't have. We even bought silly things like new shoes and clothes we didn't need just to try to be normal.

Close to new year's 2007 Ali went for a 3 day trial in a local takeaway, this would have worked great and gave us that extra cash we needed but he didn't get offered the job. We suspected the takeaway used him as free labour in the busy period, we were both worried about what our future would hold. We were in our own little world but money was running out fast, I would ring home from time to time and listen to mum plead with me to come home. She assumed Ali was holding me prisoner, she even told me to just slip out one day and come home on the train when Ali is at work. I was stunned at first but then I began to realise, no one understood this was my choice, it was what I wanted. I wasn't being brainwashed or tricked, why was that so hard to understand?

One day I agreed to go home to visit my family and talk things out, Ali was brave enough to let me go myself. His friends and extended family who had heard would call him and say, 'she won't come back, what will you do? Your izzat will be finished, don't let her go as you've done this thing now'. Ali trusted me and knew our relationship was strong, I couldn't be swayed that easily and who were they to start offering advice now. He dropped me off at the train station and I waved goodbye, it was a strange feeling as I wasn't sure what I was going home to. My uncle picked me up from the station and drove me home, there was complete silence the whole way. I had assumed dad couldn't face picking me up and I could understand why. As I stood at my front door, I felt sick, scared I didn't know how to face them. As I entered the atmosphere was different, dad was on his way to the airport to pick up his business partner who had just come back from hajj. He didn't even look at me, he couldn't if he wanted to and I felt so ashamed, my own dad couldn't even give me a glance but he told mum that he would speak to me when he got back.

Everyone was lined up in the kitchen ready to fire questions at me, Boroaffa was shocked and upset that I didn't give her a heads up about my plans. My uncle and auntie started questioning me, 'Who is this boy that you have disgraced your family for? What does he do? What will you do?' They told me Ali was lying to me, they knew how these things worked and had seen it all before, he never liked me or loved me. He was using me to get a red passport to become a British citizen as up until now he was a failed asylum seeker student. I tried to ignore them, I didn't want to believe what they said, it hurt every single word of it but naturally doubt began to run through my mind although I didn't let them know it. I answered all their questions for hours but they refused to accept me and Ali, 'What about your sisters? Who will marry your sisters if you marry this boy?' I kept looking at the time, the last train back to Leicester was at 11pm and I couldn't miss it. They even bought over my Bengali next door neighbour Mrs Khan whom I knew well and respected as she was my Bengali School teacher. My days at Bengali school were fun, whilst being taught it was a chance to get out the house and make friends with locals, chat with the girls and I even started to use it as an excuse to meet Ali shortly before I left.

Mrs Khan explained a similar situation that had happened in her family and how it ruined them. I told them this would be different and would not ruin anything but they wouldn't listen and it was already past 11pm. I was to stay until dad got back so I could speak to him, I tried to explain to dad but I knew no one would listen, I had enough I couldn't get them to understand, they had already made their minds up. Dad's business partner was a friend of the family, I knew him well and grew up playing with his daughter. He tried to tell me what I was doing was wrong, clearly dad had filled him in on the way home from the airport and he tried to do his bit. I left the living room and went upstairs to speak to my siblings one last time. I didn't know what to do, how do I go back to Leicester at this time of night. I thought about getting a taxi, but it would be way too expensive. They kept saying 'your dad will drop you off', yeah right I thought, I didn't even tell them the truth about where I was staying. I had lied and said Birmingham as I was afraid of what they might do to Ali if they found him.

I decided to ring Shafi a good friend of Ali's who had been there for us and gave us both lifts around previously. Without telling him what was going on I asked if he could pick me up and take me to Leicester, he didn't hesitate. He was working as a takeaway delivery driver at the time on a job but left his shift to drop me off. I somehow said my goodbyes to my siblings and started to head down the main road to meet Shafi, I was in a daze thinking about what just happened and what if anything had been achieved from the visit. He picked me up within five minutes, I was so grateful to him, what a true friend to Ali as I knew not many would do this. The whole journey back I sat in silence with tears streaming down my face, I didn't know what was going on anymore, I just wanted to go back to Ali, him to embrace me and tell me everything would be okay and that's exactly what happened.

We tried to lead a normal as possible life in Leicester, we ordered pizza and watched movies, but we knew this couldn't last and wasn't really normal. We tried to do our Nikah but no local Imam in the vicinity was willing to conduct the ceremony without either of our parents present because of my age and the situation. After the next week Ali sat me down, he gave me that serious look and said,

'We have to go back to Northampton Jaan'. I couldn't believe the words coming out of his mouth, 'no way' I replied. I told him he could go on his own but I was not going back with him, I feared what they would do to him if we were to go back. Deep down I knew it was the right thing to do and after much encouragement I agreed to go back and Shafi came down to pick us up, we packed all our things and drove back down to Northampton. We stayed in a rented shared house where Ali's brother Noor was staying, he gave us his room and moved in with the guy in the next room, it was very kind of him. Although Noor was shocked about what we did he wasn't a busybody and just let us get on with it, trying to help us in any way he could. Although I was very reluctant to return it felt good to be back in well-known surroundings as I was born and have always lived in Northampton and Ali had spent a good few years here too. We tried to sleep that night for what was about to come but nothing could prepare us.

Homecoming Nightmare

The next day we decided I would go back home one more time to visit my family and let them know I was back here to stay with Ali. I knew they would see or hear from someone else otherwise that I was back and I owed them that much, maybe it would show them that we were serious. Even after what happened last time I was in a dream world and thought they would invite him round to meet and get to know him but I was very wrong. I approached home again, the first door was open to the main door so I rang the doorbell with a huge lump in my throat, I entered my house of 16 years but it felt alien to me. I explained to mum that I was living with Ali in Northampton, she refused to accept what I was saying and told me to go away. 'If you want to live like this do it away from us, you've already caused us this much pain and shamed your father. Now he won't even be able to walk with his head up in the street. If you stay here your dad will kill him, he'll hurt this man', I was terrified. This is exactly what I feared would happen if we came back and as terrified as I was, I believed it.

She was raging with anger, my uncle and auntie calmed her down and tried to come to an understanding with me. My Auntie made a proposition, 'you can marry this boy but only after your two elder sisters are married. In the meantime, you can ring him once a month under supervision and can live in our house if you don't feel comfortable coming back here'. They fed thoughts into my head, 'do this for your sisters, who will marry them if you run off with this boy? think about them, don't be selfish'. My head was spinning, I didn't come here to make a deal, simply to tell them out of respect that we were back. Thoughts started processing in my head, will they really allow this? Should I agree to it? They told me that if I agree to the proposition then I was to come back home with my things by midnight and if I didn't come back by then they would assume I didn't agree and didn't want anything to do with me.

When I went back to tell Ali, it felt like a fairy tale gone wrong, be back before the clock strikes midnight, like a real-life Cinderella. I started to tell myself this was the only way to keep both my family and Ali in my life. I thought it was the right thing to do, Ali could see this proposition for what it was but he stood by me, 'it's your decision, do what your heart tells you'. I was stuck, on one side was Ali and on the other side was my family, I was being asked to choose between the two. After much deliberation with myself I decided to agree to their conditions, I thought it was for the best for everyone and I would speak to Ali soon. As the clock ticked Ali began packing my stuff for me as he could see I didn’t have the mental strength to do it myself. It still didn't feel right, I didn’t want to leave him, was I really doing this? It soon hit 11.30pm and we had to make a move although from our place to my parents was barely a 5 minute walk. ‘I’ll drop you off at the end of the street' he said, as he picked up my bags and reached for the door I fell on my knees and pleaded with him to let me stay. I was so confused, tears ran down my face as I sobbed and persisted with him that I didn't want to go back home. At this point he knew it was over and there was an extremely slim chance I would see him again, this was not a proposition it was a ploy. He reasoned with me to and tried to reassure me it was good for my sister’s future, that I was doing the right thing and we would speak soon.

He walked me up to the top of the street and waited as I walked down towards my house and left without looking back, I didn't even know what I was doing, it was happening but it didn’t feel real. I walked through the front door, put my stuff down while mum and dad hugged me. I was still in shock this didn't feel right but I knew it would take time, everyone sat down and tried to act as normal as possible. Dad was ill at the time, he had man flu and he's the type of man who never stopped going no matter what so it had to be bad for him to be at home on the sofa. Everyone forced me to have dinner, rice and curry, how could I eat after what I had done? It’s a bit of a cliché but you soon come to learn in Asian households you are often fed nonstop regardless of your refusal, that just means more food will arrive in front of you. I guess it’s kind of a comfort thing especially in a situation like this when nothing else felt normal. I felt sick, thinking about what Ali must be going through.

Dad asked me to eat with him so I sat on the sofa and fed him rice and curry with a spoon whilst I took a bite in between to please him. The whole time I couldn't stop thinking about Ali, what had I done? As I sat with dad I felt my phone vibrate, I went to the bathroom to pick it up, it was Ali.

His voice croaked as he whispered, 'I miss you Jaan, I love you, and I should never have let you go'

Hearing that from him felt like a huge weight lifted, it's like I wanted this to happen. As he spoke I realised I made a grave mistake trying to please everyone, how did I leave the man I loved? I agreed to come back and told him to wait for me at the top of my street, if I turned up then great but if I wasn't there in 30 minutes then that meant there was trouble. It was risky but I couldn't do it, I loved him and my family but it was a different kind of love.

I was petrified, how was I going to get out? Should I sneak out or should I tell them? How would I take my stuff? I went back downstairs and stood at the lounge door whilst they all talked about me.

'I can't do this' I blurted out, they all looked at me. 'I don't want to live my life like this, I love Ali and I need to be with him now.'

They told me to stop being silly and forget him but they looked at me and realised that I meant it. 'He rang you, didn't he? 'said mum. 'He told you something that's why you're saying this, he threatened you, what did he say?'

'Nothing' I shouted 'I've changed my mind, you don't understand, I want to be with him'. They all looked at me as though I was mad but they knew I was serious. I moved towards the lounge door to get to the hall and out the front door but it was slammed in my face. Mum ran over, shut the door and stood in front of it. There was a lump in my throat, they weren't going to let me go quietly. I didn't even think this could happen otherwise I would've crept out later, how could I have been so stupid? 'No, you're not going anywhere' shouted mum. 'What has he done to you? What has he told you to make you do this?' I could not understand why they couldn't see this was my choice. They sat me down, dad tried to persuade me to change my mind, whilst mum stood at the door watching me. My auntie and uncle just sat in shock, whilst tears streamed down my face. I had never been scared in my life in the presence of my family before, I just wanted to get out but I couldn't.

Dad tried to hug me, tell me I was his little girl and everything would be okay. I stood up and tried to push my mum away from the door, 'leave me alone' I cried, just let me go' but it was no use. It was around 2am now by this time, Ali had rung me half hour earlier and was waiting for me. My phone started buzzing nonstop in my pocket, I knew they would take it away from me as soon as I tried to answer it so I didn't bother to try. Dad was sick of it buzzing, 'it's him, isn't it?' he shouted. He grabbed the phone off me as I pulled it out of my pocket. That was my only way out I thought, what would I do now? I could not believe I was practically a prisoner in my own home, after a while there was knocking at the front door and the doorbell rang. They all knew it was Ali and grabbed me down on the sofa as I tried to go to the window to call out. I knew they would never hurt me but they just dint want this to happen, I cried out to Ali to help me. Dad panicked and rang someone from the restaurant, he told them to come to the house with a few others to warn Ali off. The restaurant was literally a 5 minute walk so a 2 minute run at best, I knew he didn’t have much time if they did come or maybe dad made it up to scare us. 'No' I screamed, 'leave him alone'. Dad then rang my cousin from London and tried to get me to speak to him, to try to see his point of view and talk some sense into me. I wasn't interested, I was terrified of what they might do to Ali but he carried on thumping at the front door. Ali saw a few Asian lads walking up the street in the distance, he wasn’t daft he knew what they were coming for and began to turn around and walk back up the street in the opposite direction. He walked off slowly so they wouldn’t clock on that it was him as they were coming to beat up a guy they had never met, so this way he couldn’t easily be spotted. The lads came to the house and rang dad to tell him they couldn't find Ali, the news was some comfort to me but dad was furious.

Ali went back home to the house in Lea road and called the police over and over again to explain what had happened and that he was worried about my safety but they persisted in claiming they were too busy, it wasn't urgent and they would get around to it when they could. As I sat in the lounge crying, shouting and trying to get out they were trying to tell me lies about Ali to make me change my mind but I didn’t listen or react. At about 4am they decided to call it a night, mum showed me up to her room whilst dad locked both front doors and kept the keys safe. Dad tried to talk to me sweet and softly like normal but I knew he was fuming inside. 'Get some sleep now' said mum, she told me to lie next to her. How could I sleep? I felt sick, scared, terrified in my own house of the situation I was in and what might happen? As I lay their mum asked me dozens of questions and tried to talk to me nicely. I could hear the landline ringing downstairs on repeat, it was Ali trying to get through, I smiled inside but eventually dad pulled the plug out. Ali then proceeded to the police station, they wouldn't help him and gave him the same excuses as earlier so he sat outside the corner of the station and tried to flag police cars down to help but it was no use, they were too busy. It was January, freezing cold outside, he managed to find a wall vent with some warm air creeping through at the back of the station and sat in front of it drifting in and out of sleep until daylight continuing to attempt to flag down the police.

I somehow managed to fall asleep and woke up to find mum and dad gone, everyone awake. I was annoyed with myself, how did I fall asleep, I wanted to try to get out whilst everyone slept but I must have been tired beyond belief following the events of the last 24 hours. I ran downstairs to find mum in the kitchen making breakfast whilst dad was pacing up and down the hall with my phone in his hand. I begged him to give me the phone but he refused, 'just one minute, please Abba' I cried. Soon there was a knock at the door, both mum and dad went to answer it as I peered down from the top of the stairs. Ali was stood there, my heart throbbed as I charged down the stairs, he looked at me and saw the fear in my eyes, as I tried to go towards him mum pulled the hood of my jacket to stop me and pull me back.

'What do you want?' dad asked.

'Just let her go' replied Ali. Dad told him he was mad, that he had performed black magic on me to make me do these things. He shouted at Ali and managed to accidentally hit him on his forehead with the keys in his hand as he pointed at him to go away. Dad shut the door in his face, I just wanted to get my hands on a phone to make a call to get any kind of help and get out. I scrambled around looking for a phone to make contact but it was no use, I wasn't exactly going to find a phone hanging around in that house. To my luck 15 minutes later there was a loud knock at the door. 'It's the Police, open up please', they shouted, dad looked at mum as he told her to open the door, he knew it was over. Mum pleaded with me not to tell the police anything or tell them Ali was bothering me and to take him away. Two female police officers entered, one questioned me and the other my dad, after I explained what had happened she asked me if I wanted to press charges against dad. 'No, not all' I replied, I just need to get out of here. One officer accompanied me up to my room to collect my things and took me out to the car where Ali was waiting. I had never been happier to see him, she put my things in the car boot and drove us back home to Lea Road.

After all the home coming drama we were so happy to be back together again. Life had to go on as normal as can be but times were tough and neither of us were working although we were staying in a rented room at £60 a week. We were both desperately searching for jobs and in the meantime submitted a claim for housing benefits/income support. As neither of us were in education any longer we weren't receiving monies that we used to get as an incentive for staying in school, EMA they used to call it. Ali's brother who lived in Lea road also had no permeant British residency, he worked in a local takeaway and would bring food for us every day for dinner. We would eat next to nothing throughout the day and look forward to the one guaranteed meal that would come most evenings, sometimes he would work into the very early hours so we would wait for the food to come although we got used to sleeping on an empty stomach. It got to a point where we were down to our last £60 to pay the rent for one more week and had no idea what we were going to do next.

Ali would buy this sponge, raisin cake with any change that he had in his pockets from the local shop. It was a blue packet of six mini sponge style cakes that he'd bring me with some tea. When I would ask him why he wasn't eating he would say he wasn't hungry or that he had already eaten some on the way but he knew our situation and thought as a man he could be strong and survive on nothing but had to feed me. This is one thing he'd always do to put me first, I mean who was I?, just some girl he'd met barely a year ago but today all we had was each other and the clothes on our back and I loved him for it. Luckily within that same week due to calls made by a lovely lady at the job centre on behalf of Ali some of our benefit claim had gone through and we started receiving some money. The lady in question was someone who knew Ali and helped him with a few bits when he first came to the country, like help with opening a bank account and applying for college, she was a good woman and could see the situation we were in so used her influence to get our claim processed with some urgency. To this day I don't know what would have happened otherwise, prior to that to raise some funds we sold some of our things, a portable DVD player and a few DVDs we traded in at CEX, that money helped us with our last week of rent. We were both doers and hated not working or studying, as time passed we both frantically searched for jobs but it looked bleak.

Back on Track?

Ali's brother Noor had put a few good words in for him at local takeaways but nobody had any vacancies or maybe they did but just didn't want to employ a wanted man encouraging trouble? Whichever it was, it wasn't looking good. After a few weeks Ali had a call from a man named Idris in a local takeaway, they needed someone in general to help in the shop. Ali already had plenty of previous experience so they took him on for a trial and shortly after offered him a position. It was small money and long hours however we were relieved to be getting back on track. I had joined up with about every single employment agency there was but wasn't getting anywhere, I was starting to lose hope. When I was leaving home, I managed to take my passport with me and even remembered to take my GCSE certificates too as I knew I may need them. Eventually I got a call for an interview as a sales office assistant in a computer supplies company based about 5 miles away from us. After two interviews, I was offered the job and was glad to be finally bringing some money home for us.

Soon after we both started working we decided we needed a new place to live, somewhere closer to town and we wanted to give Noor his room back. We went to view a room in a shared house as that is still all we could afford at the time, the landlord Gurdip was friendly, the house was reasonably clean and it was close to the bus station. With minimal hesitation, we paid 2 weeks deposit and moved in a week later. Things were going well, me and Ali were both working full time, we had money to spend on ourselves and didn't have to worry about what anyone thought or would say. I was getting more into my role at the computer supplies company, it was a small office and sometimes the atmosphere was quite catty whilst there was a lot of gossip and nastiness which I didn't like. The office was dominated by target and sales driven people hungry to hit targets and be the top performer. Ali was doing well but working ridiculously long hours, I was thankful that we both had jobs however we were not spending a lot of time together.

Ali had a chat with his manager as by this time he was practically running the shop single handed, they agreed to give him a fixed day off and increase his wages. Even when he was at work we chatted for hours on the phone but sometimes I still felt lonely, I had been so used to being in a house full of people at home. By Christmas time that year I was applying for a new job as I didn't particularly enjoy mine at the computer supplies company and wasn't getting paid a lot for what I was doing. I would work late and try my best to develop but no one was noticing or really cared. After a few interviews, I got a job in banking for a Building Society. I was so glad to get away from the other place I didn't even ask about the salary but it turned out to be a generous promotion which helped us greatly. I started my new job at the Society, everyone was so kind and friendly, my team were like a little family that looked after each other. There was Margaret- Mother Hen, Lynn- the wild/funny one, Mary- Mental Mary we used to call her which she didn't mind as she knew she was a bit bonkers and then there was Debbie- The sweet, lovely, sensible one who treated me as a daughter. They were all older ladies and all mothered me but Deb was too good to me, she was just always there to offer a hand and I can never repay her for her genuine kindness towards us.

Things were going well for us, Ali even surprised me one day and bought a tv from a local second-hand shop but as we had no car he carried it 3 miles home, we laughed about it the next day as he told me the story of having to stop a few times on the way but he was determined to try to give me the little things that he knew I was missing but I wouldn't mention.

Until one day Ali rang me whilst I was at work; he had been to see his solicitor Nazreen who had been handling his case since 2004 when he entered the country. He told me to come home and that he needed to tell me something. I was worried and confused, I didn't really understand much about immigration law and wasn't sure what it all meant. He told me that after his discretionary leave to remain in the country had expired he applied for further leave and this had been refused. I felt sick, I'd just ran away from everything I knew for this man and now they wanted to take him away from me too? I fell into his arms and sobbed whilst he tried to be strong and reassure me, I felt like I was losing him all over again. Over the coming days we discussed and decided to appeal against this decision using a different law firm recommended by Ali's boss as Nazreen couldn't really take this any further. His boss had been in a similar situation when he first came to the country and they won their appeal through this firm so it sounded like the right thing to do. It was difficult as the new firm were based in London and it meant a visit there every so often and time off to do this, we submitted the appeal and tried to continue living a normal life.

I started to take driving lessons and passed my theory test after a few attempts. Things were going good again, Ali used to ring his family every so often and send a little money that we could their way as we couldn't go visit them due to his status in the country. He had told them everything about me and what had happened, all they said was to ask for my dad's forgiveness and if Ali was happy then they were happy. His dad was just a little upset that Ali hadn't asked for his advice, 'I wouldn't have stopped you my son' he said, 'it's good to ask your elders for advice at times like these that's all'. I was in awe of his family's reaction, the complete opposite to mine although I can appreciate as the girl's side it was always going to be more dramatic. I couldn't believe it, considering they are Pashtun Afghans too whom I thought were a lot stricter in these situations. I heard all about his family and used to hear him speak to them in Pashtu,

I couldn't understand what was being said and often tried to work out some of the words but it's such a difficult language that I couldn't decipher it even if I tried.

Ali learnt to drive and his friend Shafi got him a job as a delivery driver in another takeaway with better hours and pay. We started to enjoy life more, we spent time together, went for dinners, cinema, shopping and all sorts. However, at the back of both our minds lay the uncertainty of how long this would last because of Ali's status in the country and the ongoing appeal we had submitted. We visited the solicitors in London when we needed to, often to make a payment, we were fighting Ali's case on human rights grounds- the right to a family life but it seemed we were not really getting anywhere. The solicitors firm turned out to be lazy and un interested in us, often failing to submit documents or keep to deadlines but I wasn't sure what other option we had. People from my community who knew about our situation often told me to have a kid with Ali, surely that would secure him a place here, they said it as if it was so easy and laughed at us trying to follow the system. I did consider it but it was not an option, I didn't want to have kids just to get my husband in the country, that's ridiculous, that's not a reason to start a family? Where would we stay? How would we support a child? and what if it didn't work, then what? I would be stuck on my own with a child and the father being taken away, no it wasn't right, it wasn't for us right now. I wanted a child out of happiness and when the time was right, not in a desperate situation out of need.

We approached Nazreen, Ali's solicitor again for some un biased friendly advice on the pending appeal. She told us based on the file and history the chances of the appeal being successful were very slim. I began to read up and educate myself on the home office rules and immigration matters, the more I read the more it frightened me.

Back to black

We both knew Ali's appeal to remain in the UK was not going anywhere and just pro longing the inevitable, I guess we just ignored the truth for a while and tried to be hopeful. Until one day we were just chatting casually and Ali said to me, 'Jaan we need to think of the best way forward for our future'. I looked at him puzzled as I didn't want to confront the ugly truth, I was content with what we had and didn't want things to change but deep down I knew this wasn't a secure position we were in. We decided that Ali would voluntarily go back to Afghanistan then I would follow and we would marry there, I'd meet his family and I would come back to the UK and sponsor him back over as my husband. Thinking back now we were both so naive and thought it sounded like a fool proof plan, let's just say the phrase 'easier said than done' applies here. The thought of me being on my own made me feel sick, I had just turned 18 years old and had to grow up fast but I didn't want all those responsibilities. Ali never did the whole bend down on one knee proposal although we both just knew we wanted to spend our lives together and made a mutual decision to marry. I guess the day we ran away was the day he proposed and I accepted. I was terrified of Ali's proposal to go back to Afghan but knew it was the right thing to do. We booked our tickets and spent the remaining months making the most of the time together, we worked hard making money for the flights, wedding and his visa application.

We went to see Nazreen to withdraw his appeal to demonstrate that he was voluntarily leaving the country rather than just being rejected and made to leave, this would add credibility to our case or so we hoped. As a result, Ali had to make visits to Bedford to sign in every month at the immigration centre as they were keeping a close eye on him now he made them aware of his intent to leave. His friends were astonished with his decision but nevertheless supportive and somewhat envious as many of them had not been back home for many years due to their status in the country being in limbo, waiting around years for the outcome of a case that some never received. Some of them with wives and children, watching them grow up through pictures sent if they were lucky and phone calls. The time came when I had to tell my work colleagues exactly what my situation was as I needed a month off work to travel to Afghan. Alhamdulilah they were so good to me and although shocked they supported me in any way they could. It made me think of how good these strangers were to me as oppose to my own who turned their back for their own reasons but it hurt. I was closest to Debbie who was also my senior advisor, I took her in a meeting room and just blurted it all out. As an English lady at first, I thought she would think I was stupid or crazy, or just a typical Asian girl marrying someone I was promised to but to my surprise she didn't judge me one bit. I cried into her arms and she consoled me, she told me she thought I was brave and strong for what I was doing and that she would support me all the way.

It felt like a weight had been lifted and I could discuss things openly at work whilst little did I know Debbie would more than keep her promise. We decided to fly to Afghan separately, I would fly 2 weeks after Ali to give him a chance to re unite with his family, explain and gage their reaction after being away from them 5 years. What I didn't think much about was me, an 18 year old girl who had barely left her own town forget country flying to an alien country/potential war zone alone and not even a direct flight but we didn't have much choice.

Before leaving we needed to print documents and copies of things to take with us to submit for the application, we came across an Islamic store in town which also had a few computers with internet and printing facilities. The shop was run by an English revert lady Zahira and her family, it was lovely to see a hidden gem like this amongst all the craziness and hustle and bustle of retail shops in town. She also had café facilities and sold tea, coffee, samosas and cake, there was also an area to pray at the back of the shop. It was such a calm and peaceful place, we would visit regularly to use the internet and for a while we were just like any other customer. Zahira was a friendly and engaging lady, she would always make polite conversation with us and sometimes I could see her wondering about us, this clearly very young couple coming in and using the internet so often. We got chatting and as they say the rest was history, she got to know about our situation and was intrigued and ready to help in any way she could.

The day for Ali to fly home came around quick, I made him eggs for breakfast and watched him eat as he tried to get me to eat with him but I felt sick at him leaving I couldn't even look at food right now. We sat waiting for Shafi to pick him up and take him to the airport, I tried to be strong but it was hard, I couldn't help but wonder if this was the right thing to do. He gave me a big hug and told me everything would be ok, not to worry. He began to take his cases down the stairs without a second look, tears raced down my face as I tried to wipe them away. I ran back to our room and threw myself on the bed, I tried to keep busy and turned the TV on, it was a weekend so EastEnders Omnibus was on. I stared at the screen thinking about what had just happened, would I ever see him again? Would he still love me? How would I cope on my own? My stomach was in knots and my mind was numb, my eyes hurt from crying so I tried to take a nap.

He rang me when he got to the airport, 'it doesn't feel real' I told him,

' I know Jaan', he explained he couldn't look back because he wouldn't be able to stop crying if he did. The next day was Monday and I went to work feeling numb, but glad I could try to keep occupied whilst Ali was on the second leg of his journey from Pakistan to

Afghanistan. This is because you can't fly directly to Afghanistan from the UK so you have to transit through another country. Ali rang me late afternoon the same day to let me know he had arrived home. I felt somewhat at ease that he had arrived safely but on the other hand it meant that was it, he was gone, I had let him go. I thought about how his family would react to me, Was it all an act? Would they try to persuade him to leave me? I didn't know anything about the country or culture, would our relationship be accepted?

I had only ever flown once before to Bangladesh and that was 10 years ago with my family. I was scared and felt vulnerable but was just looking forward to seeing Ali so much, it felt like we had been apart months but it had only been 2 weeks. Ali told me his family were fine about it all, they had just heard some false rumours about me from people that they were a bit concerned about but he put their mind at rest. He showed them a picture of me and they were excited to meet me in person, it was such a relief to hear and encouraging as they could have easily reacted like others but they chose not to, I greatly respected them for this and the excitement grew.

Mujhse Shaadi Karoge- Will you marry me?

The big day finally came, I was flying out to Ali and his family, all I had to do was pack my case and be ready whilst Shafi would take me to the airport. Before Ali left we went to Luton to buy a wedding outfit and accessories for myself as I wouldn't really be able to or have time to shop for it in Afghan. Ali knew it wouldn't be the same big fancy, expensive wedding that most girls dream of, my family were not there to see me off and we didn't have a lot of money to spend but he still wanted me to feel special. I chose a turquoise blue colour lengha with pink work covered in heavy gold embroidery, I have always loved looking around all the Asian shops since I was little, all the beautiful colours, dazzling jewels and beautiful patterns. There were only a few Indian clothes shops in Northampton which didn't have a lot of choice and they tended to rip you off hence the trip to Luton. I also purchased some jewellery and sparkly sandals to complete the outfit along with a few plain shalwar kameez to take with me for daily wear. When we were bargaining a price for the lengha the shop keeper supposed Ali was my family, 'Go on brother, treat your sister and take it for this final price'. We both giggled to ourselves at the reality but could appreciate his misunderstanding at our relationship as it was not the norm at all for fiancé's in our culture to go wedding shopping together.

On the way to the airport Shafi told me about the Afghan culture, how I was to greet people and what would be expected of me. He was a good guy & friend to Ali who understood our situation without question when others failed to. It made me think of something in the Afghan culture called Pashtunwali which is a very old non-written ethical code & lifestyle which the Pashtun people follow. It's a code of honour, under this even if your enemy visited your house you would protect and be hospitable to them as a courtesy of the Pashtun people which they genuinely still abide by today. Anyway, I arrived at London Heathrow airport in good time and started my 7 hr journey to Afghanistan with the connecting flight in Islamabad-Pakistan.

When I arrived in Islamabad I wasn't allowed to leave the airport because I was a transit passenger with no visa for Pakistan but I needed to get to Ali as for some reason the ticket from Pakistan to Afghan was a paper ticket retrievable from the Pakistan International Airline office in Islamabad only. Ali managed to get to Pakistan and grab it for me but of course he had to give it to me to travel. I managed to find him in the crowds of the waiting area having explained my situation to the immigration officer whom I was escorted out with to meet him. I met Ali's cousin Hassan for the first time which was nerve racking as it was the first person from his family I was to meet but it was fine he literally just said hello and smiled. Ali was allowed to come into the PIA waiting lounge so we had lunch together whilst waiting for my next flight and chatted. I wanted to hug him when I saw him but knew it wasn't appropriate in the airport so somehow I refrained, eventually it was time for me to check in for my next flight and Ali was to leave and start his journey back to Afghan too but he was going by car and I was going by plane which was a difference of a forty five minute plane vs a 5 hour car journey.

As I flew over the Afghan mountains, everything looked so desert like and different but nevertheless it was calm and tranquil. I didn't know what to expect as all you see on the television is the media influenced side of Afghanistan. The Taliban and corruption however the Afghanistan I could see was beautiful snow topped mountains, clear air and rows of colourful flowers. I met an Afghani lady sitting beside me on the flight to Kabul, she could read the excitement and anxiety on my face and started chatting with me in Urdu. I could understand Urdu from watching Indian films at home but couldn't speak a lot so I replied in English. To my surprise she also replied in perfect English, I felt at ease a little as she could relate and was the closest thing to the UK I knew at that time. As we got chatting she asked me where I was from and who I was visiting in Afghan, I gave her the short version of our story so far and all she said was

'Don't worry, one day inshallah your parents will understand'.

When I got to Kabul, Ali's brother Javed would pick me up as Ali was still on his way back from Pakistan by road. The lady I met had kindly offered me her phone to ring Javed however I didn't have his number which I know was very silly. Going through immigration in Kabul airport was an experience, as I handed over my passport with the valid visa inside I could tell by the look on the officer's face that he was wondering what the hell a British born girl is doing travelling to Afghan on her own, almost intrigued but concerned at the same time. I managed to grab my luggage off the belt and avoid the people trying to offer to push your luggage for you for a small fee. As I walked towards the crowd of people in the heat I saw a sign and on it was written 'HAFIA', I laughed to myself at the clear error. As I drew closer he quickly disposed of the sign and walked towards me, offering me a handshake, it was Ali's brother Javed and he could speak good English, great I thought.

'Salaam Sister, how are you and how was your journey'? he asked.

'Walaikum Salaam, alhamdulilah I am well and I have arrived safely' I answered.

'Who is this woman with you?' he whispered.

'She's a kind lady I met on the plane who helped me', I replied. He looked at her with a sigh of relief, he later told me he thought she was my mother and that I had brought her with me for support. I laughed at this knowing the sad reality that I had not seen or spoken to my family in months.

On the car journey home we chatted generally, he asked about my flight and what my perceptions of Afghanistan were. Along with Javed came two of Ali's sisters to the airport, I tried to communicate with them as best I could but they were equally busy smiling and observing me. My attention was towards the view out of the window, bustling markets, children on bicycles, busy traffic and tooting horns on the roads with no care or concern for others, I felt a sense of freeness. The mountains stood tall in the sandy, dusty surroundings, there was just so much going on, so much to look at and listen to. The journey to Ali's house felt like a long one but I didn't mind as I was intrigued by the country and things that I had never seen before. Javed joked with me as we drove past a huge mountain telling me the family house was at the top of this mountain and we'd have to climb by foot, I laughed nervously but part of me wondered if he was serious. I hope not I thought, not in these heels, I won't make it. We arrived by late afternoon pulling up to a big one storey brick house in the middle of open fields, as I stepped out of the car I was led to a big blue metal door. There was soft folk music playing, people talking and a gentle breeze to counteract the harsh sun beaming in the sky, as I walked in trying to keep my composure I was mesmerised by it all.

Javed led me into a room, I walked in and sat down on the floor as there were no sofas here. Traditionally Afghans have big cushion like floor seating, no chairs or sofas although that didn't stop it looking grand and formal, I wasn't surprised by this as Ali had mentioned this to me before and as a Muslim it is a sunnat to sit on the floor and eat. Floor seating is also quite traditional in Arabic country households as they find it more comfortable, their version of a sofa. There were a lot of women standing in a big circle staring at me, I felt a little intimidated although they were all smiling at me trying to ease my nerves. I was introduced to each one, I knew there was no way I would remember all the names there were just too many, they all hugged and kissed me as we were introduced.

Javed's wife was pregnant at the time and he started joking about that and how many children he already had. We all sat and chatted but it was a lot to take in and they noticed the anxious and slightly frightened expression on my face. I wasn't scared but just wanted to see Ali, a familiar face to put myself at ease in these somewhat alien surroundings, but I knew he was on his way. After some time, Ali rang Javed to check I made it there ok, they decided to play a prank on him and told him they couldn't find me at the airport and that I hadn't turned up. At first Ali was concerned but as he made his way home I think he knew it was a just a cruel joke. I played along as I didn't want to cause any issues, I hid in Javed's room when Ali came and I could hear them fooling around with him but he wasn't having any of it. Eventually I came out and saw him, I signed with relief, I felt so much better with a familiar face around. That night we all had dinner and went to bed early as we were both exhausted from travelling.

The next day was 22nd July 2008, the day of our Nikah, although we had been living together in the UK for some time we had tried to marry in Leicester when we left home but no Imam was prepared to conduct the ceremony. Ali's family invited their Imam round from their local mosque to complete the Nikah at home. Although it seemed very quick considering we had only arrived the day before it had to be done as soon as possible as currently our relationship was not halal.

Me and Ali already decided we would marry when we were in the UK so I was fine with it, Javed was in one room with me and all the women so he could translate whilst Ali was in another with the Imam and all the men. In Islam if a woman tries to marry without the permission of her parents her marriage would be invalid however there is a workaround so to speak. Ali's brother in law, Faisal who was a bit younger than my dad became my Nikah father and took the responsibilities of my father so I could marry. Faisal's responsibilities wouldn't end there and he couldn't treat me as a daughter purely for the sake of the marriage, he would effectively have to treat me the same as his birth daughters from now on. It was a big responsibility and I really appreciated his willingness to take this on for a girl he had effectively just met. Javed was going back and forth to both rooms, communicating the responses to everyone, 'Do you agree to marry Ali Khan Niazai, son of Abdul Haq Niazai?' he asked awaiting my response. I looked around hesitating for a minute, trying not to act too keen, 'Qubool hai' I replied. 'Qubool hai' I repeated twice more in line with the requirement to ensure the witnesses heard me agreeing of my own accord and this was communicated back to the Imam and Ali, with that the marriage was complete. We had bought a wedding ring set from the UK which we were already wearing, they were nothing special just a set of £100 gold band rings with a simple design engraved on from Argos to symbolise the marriage, as in Islam there is no requirement to exchange rings.

It was not a conventional ceremony but still a happy one none the less and finally the festivities could begin, our being together could be properly celebrated. Ali's eldest sister in law dressed in a traditional Afghan kuchi dress and had a little dance whilst others played drums in celebration. Every time Ali's brother Javed came into the room she would run and hide under the bed then come back out when he left as women shouldn't dance in the presence of certain men. I sat smiling as all the ladies sang and danced in happiness feeding each other sweets to celebrate. After a while Ali came and sat with me, we chatted about how it felt now that we were properly married, although nothing had really changed it felt amazing that in the eyes of God and everyone else we were finally married.

With our Nikah ceremony being so quick and small we decided to have a joint wedding party with Ali's brother Raj who was engaged, due to marry any day now. All the men sat together, wrote the invitations and chatted about whatever men talk about when they get together whilst I sat amongst the women doing the same. Ali has two younger sisters still at home and two elder sisters who are married, along with an army of seven brothers, mashallah. Each of the married brothers & sisters have a small troop of children themselves which is typical in an Asian household as I'm sure you will have understood by now. I would talk to his younger sisters in my working progress of Urdu language that I had learnt off watching Indian films. They are lovely girls and always treated me like their own sister rather than sis in law, I couldn't believe how open and welcoming they all were. At times, I couldn't help but naturally remain a little cautious, there had to be a catch I thought so I didn't want to let my guard down just yet. Growing up I had heard stories of horrible, devious in laws treating their daughters-in-law like dirt after marriage and causing trouble. I didn't expect the treatment I was getting, no one could say a bad word and as the days went by I began to feel at ease and opened up more with everyone.

As Ali's mum and dad could only talk Pashtu, I'd sit with them and Ali's sisters would translate my Urdu to them and vice versa with their Pashtu. My father in law is just a normal, happy go lucky guy and reminded me of my dad in his tendencies and attributes. My mother in law always has a big smile on her face, we smile and laugh with each other when we struggle to understand one another but she treats me better than a daughter. Whenever I would think about the situation my heart would sink, considering these people live in a country like Afghanistan without all the modern convenience and have their own daily struggles to deal with, they don't know much about the country/culture where I have come from yet they welcome me with open arms based on their son being happy. I love and respect them so much for that and I pray god rewards them for having such big open hearts.

A little while before I left the UK I had heard of Boroaffa's marriage taking place, although of course I wasn't partial to a formal invitation it still hurt knowing I wasn't there on such a family occasion. Before I left mum and dad were searching for a match for her but hadn't had much luck as everyone just turned out to be not what they said they were. I would speak to my sisters secretly here and there, poor girls, I don't think they knew if they could or should speak to me or not. When I saw them in town one day they gave me a copy of Boroaffa's wedding DVD to watch, I cried most of the time it was playing just seeing how much everyone had grown and changed especially my brothers and cousins. It brought back to me what I was missing out on but at such a time where me and Ali were going through something ourselves which just made it worse.

All the preparation for the wedding was under way, Raj's fiancé's house was 5 minutes away and I heard he would sneak out to meet her whilst they were engaged. I thought that was cute, that something like that still happened in this country considering what we hear back in the UK about arranged marriages and just the strictness of the country itself. Ali's family bought me a beautiful blue and gold thread lengha suit in addition to a substantial gold and stone jewellery set. I felt overwhelmed, I wasn't expecting anything and it certainly wasn't necessary. The night before the wedding was the henna night, it was so vibrant and loud, all the female and male guests were separated. The men rented out a gazebo and set it up in the back yard whilst the women just came spilling out of the house. I wore the clothes Ali's family bought me and sat outside on a stage for all the ladies to see which I knew was the norm.

It was the middle of July and scorching heat, the house was soon bustling with guests, the women and children came over to take a look, ask questions and congratulate me. Ali's sisters were both on hand to translate and shoo away anyone interrogating, they were my right hand girls. I think people were shocked as they expected a girl from England naturally to be in a pair of tight jeans, no headscarf and everything hanging out. To their surprise, I was just like them, covered up, could read the Quran and had a headscarf on my head. I couldn't help but laugh at the clear shock on some of the women's faces who just couldn't believe it and were almost disappointed at my normality. The henna night went on and was a success, there was music, dancing and eating. Later I got changed into something more comfortable and a lady came in to start applying beautiful henna designs on my hands. Whilst I was hanging around I went to take a sneak peak in the men's side and to my surprise I spotted Ali dancing. I stood there and sniggered as I had never seen him dance before, well not Afghan style moves. After a few minutes, he caught me from the corner of his eyes and ran towards me embarrassed, I turned the opposite way and ran away from him giggling like a school kid. That night I lay in bed whilst I could hear the men's party continue into the early hours, after a while to my surprise the window opened and Ali jumped in, he cuddled up next to me and we fell asleep in each other's arms.

The next morning was the wedding day, the 'handover' so to speak, I wasn't sure how to feel or what to do on my wedding day as it wasn't going to be a conventional ceremony. Everyone was running around getting things ready whilst I woke up at my own pace and started to get myself ready. I didn't know much about wedding makeup at the time but had studied a few YouTube tutorials beforehand to give me some ideas, I decided on a basic gold eye with black eyeliner and a bit of blush. There was none of these false lashes, contouring & setting powder in those days, or not that I knew of anyway. After getting ready guests started to arrive, women and children were swarming the place whilst some had not left from the night before. I had a stage/seating area set up in my room upon which I sat whilst women came in, had a good look and left. I had got used to it by now from the night before, it was normal but just extra intense because I was from 'London' and there was a certain expectation. Before I knew it, it was lunch time and everyone started to eat, at that time Ali's sisters came and sat with me they bought me a plate of food to nibble on. Back in the UK all I knew of our culture at any Bengali weddings I had been to was that I would see the bride sit on the stage looking down at the ground the whole time, not making eye contact with the groom and just looking all shy and timid. Although it was a little different for me as me and Ali had been together a while respectfully I followed suit and tried to play the timid bride. To my surprise Ali's sisters asked me why I looked so sad, I explained the reasoning behind my falsified expressions. They laughed at me, 'don't worry' they said, 'you can laugh, smile and be happy all you want here we don't mind'. I was shocked but pleasantly surprised to be able to end this charade and relieve my neck ache that had been building from keeping my head down. It was mostly a day of greeting people I hadn't met before, eating and chilling, I didn't even get to see Ali till later in the day as we had already completed our Nikah so there was no rush. As the day drew to a close, Raj's new wife had entered the house, me and Ali took some pics with the family for memories and to use as supporting evidence to add with the new case we were going to submit.

It made me think about back in the UK where you would pay a photographer or videographer to take professional pictures or typically put together a wedding video. It felt strange not to have the massively grand celebration I saw back home although, I was more than happy that I was marrying the man I chose and loved. Everyone was so happy and free spirited, Ali's dad was pleased that two of his sons were officially married and his mum was just as joyed.

That night I whispered to Ali 'We made it Jaan, we are finally husband and wife, how does it feel?'

He just smiled at me with a look of content, we were both relieved not to be living in sin any longer. The next few days I spent getting to know the family, meeting relatives/elders, all the women who came would come carrying all sorts of gifts. Nuts, fruits, fresh eggs were just a selection, not to mention the sweets I got thrown over me everywhere I went which apparently is a bit of a cultural celebratory tradition. It was a bit strange at first but I soon got used to it and all the kids used to run up to me afterwards to grab the sweets, eventually when I would go somewhere new I would stand waiting for the sweets to be thrown as I knew the drill by now.

Everyone at home would sit together and eat in one place on the floor, not only because it's a Sunnah of our prophet PBUH but it was the norm and was a good opportunity for everyone to chat together. For the first few days Ali's sister would bring food to our room and we would eat separately, each brother had their own room in the house, even Ali who hadn't been back in years. Dad had recently built the house from new whilst all the brothers helped fund it and the surrounding land, the family also own 2 vineyards which was their main income and other bits of land here and there. After a couple of days, I asked Ali's sister why we ate separately, she explained they thought I would feel awkward or wouldn't like it with everyone as I was from 'London'. I laughed at their assumptions and thanked them for their concern, the following days we all sat together for meals which I preferred.

The days flew by as I got to learn a lot about this alien country, sweet people and their beautiful values & traditions. Time was running out as my return flight was approaching and we had to make our marriage official in court for it to be recognised by the Home office. Ali's eldest sister lived in the capital Kabul where we needed to travel to register the marriage so we decided to spend the night at hers. We travelled by taxi and swapped cars along the way, it is common practice to haggle a fare for a taxi with the driver before getting in so this often took some time for such a long journey. It took about an hour to get to Kabul and on the way, there were all sorts of smells & views for me to appreciate. We arrived at an official building, Ali would go in and check the place out, ask the questions and if it was ok then he called me in to avoid all the unnecessary staring and questions. Although I am of Bengali descent and my skin is pretty much the same colour as the Afghans, my facial features are supposedly quite different to the locals. I have large eyes which was not the norm here and that in conjunction with me opening my mouth to speak in English would give the game away. We were not looking to hide anything from officials but just didn't need the extra hassle from locals asking questions about what in their eyes was an English girl doing in Afghanistan. One of the first phrases I learnt in Pashtu was 'Ghat Stargee' which translates to big eyes as it was the first thing anyone I met for the first time would point out and compliment me on.

We needed three witnesses for the marriage certificate so we took along two relatives and one village elder. They all went in did their bit then me and Ali were questioned, before it came to talk of money. Although there was a fee for the service, an admin fee, they knew I was British and how important this certificate was for us, so as usual it was a bit of a game for them. Offer the best bribe and you will get what you came for, which Ali and Javed were prepared for. The certificate was issued from the local court and I began to feel at ease that things were coming along and we were soon on our way to stay the night at his sister's house before travelling back the next day. My 3 weeks in Afghanistan soon came to an end and it was time for me to return home to the UK. It was difficult leaving Ali again but in the knowledge, that he would apply and within 6 months inshallah be successful in securing a 2 yr spouse visa, I was not as anxious and remained hopeful. For an 18 year-old girl who had barely travelled, I coped quite well flying to and back on my own. It was 4 flights in total, in my case flying back via Islamabad- Pakistan. Although at times whilst travelling it was lonely on the plane, tears began to flow as I was coming to terms with leaving him again. The thought of not knowing when I would see him again was beyond tough but we had little choice.

Refused, Refused, Refused

When I returned I focused on work and would speak to Ali daily, often twice a day before and after work on the bus. He got to know the people that would get on at different stops as he would hear the same voices and sounds in the background each day. I would often reflect on the bus journey in, people watching, a young girl who also worked at the bank would play with her baby before dropping him to the crèche around the corner and the general conversations of the school kids.

I rushed to town one Saturday to get some of our wedding pictures printed, I walked into Boots and put my things down to start following the instructions on one of the photo printing screens. As I tried to continue I felt myself feel weak and black out, next thing I knew I was taken into the back room being fanned down and offered water. The assistant played the usual concern routine but I decided I was fine and shooed her away, I tried a second time to print the pictures. This time again I felt unwell and called her back, she took me to the managers room and asked me if I was in town with anyone. 'No' I replied with a hint of sarcasm knowing the reality, she refused to let me go home alone without being picked up.

Let me call your husband she demanded,

I laughed 'you'll have to dial internationally then' I replied,

'Ok well what about mum or dad, sister?' she asked innocently,

I sniggered 'no, there's no one'.

'Look if I let you go alone and anything happens to you out on the street, then you don't know what people are like, they will just walk over you, it's sad but it's true and if your lucky someone might help but I can't take that risk'. She was right and it was nice to think someone actually cared about my wellbeing. She eventually agreed to call me a taxi with strict orders to ensure the driver watched me enter the house safely. It was times like that it really brought everything home, when they ask you for next of kin on documents that you think you will never need to use but you never hesitate to answer it and put someone down, but me, my next of kin was thousands of miles away.

Ali had travelled to Pakistan to submit his application to the UK embassy as there was no facility to do this in Afghanistan. He had paid the £700 fee and submitted the application in Islamabad which included all the supporting evidence I had brought over and reams of our call records. As he waited for the outcome he stayed at his Cousins house in

Eptibad, Islamambad. He tried to keep himself busy by doing an English course to improve his grammar and speech whilst his cousins kept him company in evening. As we waited for the outcome of the application time seemed to stand still, it felt like it was taking forever although the processing timescales were expected at 8-12 weeks. Every night I would come home and check the visa update website, hoping and praying we would hear and that it would be good news.

After two months of waiting we received the news we were dreading, the application had been refused as the marriage certificate submitted was only registered from a local court as opposed to the high court. The officer did not believe it was a legitimate marriage as this type of document had basically been signed off by village elders in the local village which anyone could do. Neither of us had any idea of the need to have registered the marriage in the high court, we didn't really know there was a difference or how this would affect us.

'Look on the bright side' I said at least they haven't just refused us for no reason, maybe we do just need to sort this certificate out?' I questioned myself, was this a legitimate reason or a way to try to get a bribe out of us. We had little time to react and had to decide what our next steps were fast. I went to town to get some shopping but I would walk around jut staring at things as my mind was somewhere else, I was depressed, all I could think about was what would happen with the case and why I let Ali go. I would see couples together, laughing and joking or just acting normal, it would remind me and bring tears to my eyes, I would run home, close the door and weep to console myself. At times I felt trapped, lonely, afraid, vulnerable, what was I doing at the age of 18? The only interaction I would get with others was at work, some days when I would come home from work or at weekends I would literally not open my mouth for 24-48 hrs just because there was no one to speak to, no one to interact with but this became the norm for me.

I had already used my holiday up from work for that year so I had to wait 2 months until the next year Jan 2009. I planned to fly back out, visit Ali and sort all this marriage certificate business so he could re-apply for his 2 yr spouse visa. Between being refused and waiting to fly out again we had some devastating news, of all the things that could happen to us or go wrong at this point, the UK law had changed. The age requirement for a spouse to sponsor their partner to the UK had risen from 18 to 21, this was an attempt to protect young Asian girls from forced marriages. Our world collapsed, it's over I thought, I am being punished so badly for what I have done. What about the young girls like me who choose to marry at this age? Me and Ali were both in shock, we couldn't see a way out. My heart felt as if it had been torn apart and ripped out, I was in a daze, I couldn't eat or sleep for weeks, I was only 18 turning 19 in 4 months' time. I felt sick to my stomach every time I thought about it, was this the end of our story? I would sit and think so much that at times I would randomly cry on the bus or when I was at work, especially when I saw couples together, I wasn't asking for much was I? People talked, they tried to give me advice and told me to leave Ali, it wasn't worth it, I had done what I could but this was too much, they could never understand, they weren't living it. I didn't want them to understand, I ignored them, you can't switch love on and off, this was my life and I had to make a decision.

Eventually we decided I would leave the UK and live in Afghan until I turned 21, I had no intention of waiting 3 yrs in the UK for the man I loved with no family or real friends around me. I was about to give my notice for the room to the landlord, we hadn't discussed much about what I would do in Afghan but we couldn't see any other way. I spoke to Nazreen who agreed the law change was legal but just very unfortunate timing for us, I wrote to local MP's and the house of parliament in a bid to raise their attention to our situation and others who would also be adversely affected by this but it was no use. Eventually my Nikah father Faisal spoke to me and Ali on the phone, he had heard about our plans and felt he had a responsibility to give us some advice. He explained to us that the quality of life in Afghanistan is not what I was used to and Ali had been out of the country for so long too. He questioned what I would do in Afghan, I would get bored and it wouldn't be the same as holidaying. Also, when I would come back to the UK in 3 years' time, I would struggle to build myself up again to enable me to sponsor Ali over, finding a job, a place to live. As obvious as it seems we hadn't given all these details much thought, just the thought of being apart that long was too much for us. The more we thought about it, we knew what Faisal said made sense, we could struggle and live in difficulty for 3 yrs then enjoy the rest of our lives or be together now but struggle in Afghanistan for who knows how long. It was a difficult decision but we decided to wait the 3 yrs out and Ali would come to visit on a 6 month family visit visa when he could, it was far from ideal but in the long run it was the best choice in the unfortunate situation we found ourselves in.

I flew back out to Afghan as I planned to finish what I had started, I was excited to see Ali and focused on getting the marriage certificate right this time whilst at the back of my mind I wondered when or if realistically I would see him again for good. Previously I travelled to Afghan in the height of summer, the sweltering heat and got to enjoy the fresh ripe fruits of the season. Jan 2009 was a very different story, freezing cold and snow up to the knees was the norm whilst everyone walked around looking like eskimo's. We got to work as soon as I got there and travelled to various places to get the marriage properly certified. People turned us away, we had to bribe, beg and use contacts just to get the marriage certified properly. This is crazy, I thought, we just want what's rightfully ours, we are not asking for anything more. Every time we got knocked back was another unnecessary hurdle, we'd come back home after being out in the cold all day with nothing to show for it. Ali's family tried to keep our spirits up but we'd both come back so tired we would just curl up in the corner, by the fire and try to get some rest.

After a week of travelling to various courts, judge's houses etc in the treacherous snow we managed to get the correct stamps/certification required. I was only in Afghan for 3 weeks due to work so my time was up fast and when I returned home, Ali also returned to Pakistan and submitted the 6 month family visit visa application. There were so many agents lurking around the embassy claiming to help people for a fee or making false promises, we were tempted and had serious discussions about it but eventually decided against it. A lot of these agents would play with people's emotions, people who they knew were vulnerable and would pay them any amount when they didn't have any additional influence on the case. I did a lot of the research myself using the internet, searching forums and old court case decisions whilst also keeping in touch with Ali's old solicitor Nazreen.

Whilst we waited for the outcome of the application we both continued to make dua like no other. In addition to the daily prayers I would find myself sitting on the prayer mat every evening crying to Allah asking for his help. I don't want anything else I would cry, take everything from us but help us be together. 'Allah you are the all-knowing, if this is good for us then grant us success in this hardship we face and if it is not then grant us ease and help us be content with what we have. Ameen.' What I didn't realise at the time was that this was a test for us, a test of our love for one another and to bring us both closer to Allah as he only tests the ones he loves.

We expected the visa application to be successful this time, they refused us previously for something which we now rectified so logically what else could go wrong. This is where I got to learn that some of the individuals working in the embassy I can only describe as jealous and corrupt individuals. Ali called and broke the news, he had been refused again, more money down the drain and we were no closer to being re united. I broke down, I became weak, I didn't know what else we could do, I couldn't take much more of this. We both tried to console each other but neither of us could, we were heart broken and tired of the fight. I was a 19 year old girl having to deal with all this in addition to work and support myself and my husband whilst trying to live a normal life. I knew I chose this the minute I left my parents' house so I couldn't give up now but I felt like the world was against us.

I went to visit Nazreen, Ali's old solicitor to see if she could help on what we do next. There was an option to appeal the decision as the basis of the refusal was that they didn't think Ali would return following the 6 month visit. What a load of rubbish? We weren't stupid, why would we jeopardise him coming back to the UK permanently? Surely, we would abide by the rules as best as possible as our future intent was much greater than this so couldn't adversely affect Ali's immigration history. Nazreen was brilliant, she welcomed me with open arms and it was good to see a familiar face, someone I could trust and knew what to do in this situation. She advised that we would pledge an appeal from the UK, the reasoning they gave for the refusal was weak, the embassy case workers can be jealous people and don't want to see others have a happy ending. It was hard to believe corruption existed even in the official places but I was soon starting to learn the nature of the country and how money often dictated a lot of issues.

I didn't know what to think about the appeal although Nazreen was very positive but we had already expected the 6 month visit visa to be successful and that didn't work out so why would it now? I tried to remain hopeful but it was hard, I would speak to Ali in the morning on the bus on my way into work and on the way home. There was usually a time difference of 3-4 hrs ahead in Afghan which made it hard for me to wait until I got home to call him as it would be very late there and he would often fall asleep. Sometimes the conversations became repetitive regarding our situation and we would end up arguing over nothing, clearly both stressed and confused about everything. Calls to Afghan from the UK were at a premium of 14 pence a minute, whereas I knew in other south Asian countries it was much less. A lot of it was to do with Afghan not having any deals with any of the major UK line providers although I could understand why this wasn't a priority for a country not long out of war. The phone signal was bad in Ali's village and internet was not really an option due to an even poorer signal. I tried to limit the call times and frequency but I struggled, I couldn't be with my husband so at the least I should be able to hear his voice. I argued with myself over what I felt should be a basic human right, I knew deep down I was spending too much on calls, on average around £150-200 per month which was too much on my conservative salary. Ali would be deep in conversation and the call would get cut off as I would run out of credit, I would top up and ring back as quickly as possible telling a tale that the signal got cut off as I knew he would tell me off for spending too much on calls otherwise. We started on around 3 ten minute calls a day but had to cut them down to once a day, some days not at all due to signal issues. At times I would spend more on calling him and less on food, I could get by on anything but wanted to at least hear my husband's voice every day.

I had to make a choice at times, I knew I was only a young girl but I had to be strong and think & act like an experienced mature woman to get through this.

Within a few weeks of appeal, I received a court date, we thought this had to be a positive sign as they wouldn't allow the appeal if there was no chance. My now friend Zahira had heard about what had happened and offered to drive me to Birmingham where the appeal was being heard in court. She left her 5 children including toddler with her friend who lived locally just so she could drive me and come along for support. She is a very caring, generous woman who wears her heart on her sleeve and became a true friend we came across on our journey. We chatted generally on the way and Zahira tried to keep me optimistic and hopeful for the hearing. When we got to Court I sat in the waiting area with Nazreen, she was very positive and told me not to worry. 'Just be honest and tell the judge what's in your heart' she said. As we waited for our slot, we got to know it was a later hearing with a judge who was due to retire very shortly. I didn't know if there was any truth in this or if this was a good or bad thing but it just made me more anxious. As we entered the court room I didn't know what to expect, I had never been anywhere like this before. The home office representative introduced himself and the judge entered the room. Judge Freer, he just looked like a normal man with a wig on his head although I don't know what else I was expecting. The home office representative started with his defence, I just stared at him thinking why are you trying to ruin our lives but ultimately, I knew he had a job to do. Nazreen then did her bit as our representative, she was amazing she gave a personal character witness for Ali in addition to the general appeal as she had known him for so long having dealt with his previous case to remain in the UK. She put her job on the line and vouched for him as a professional knowing his history and that our relationship and intentions were genuine. I truly believe she was our angel in human form that Allah sent down to protect us on that day and pray inshallah that she be rewarded greatly for this as I'm certain this swung it for us.

It was quickly my turn to convince the judge our relationship and situation was genuine and that we were helpless. My stomach was in knots but I just remembered what Nazreen had said, I broke down at times as I told the judge everything from the beginning. From how we met, to my family situation and how Ali was the only person left in this world that I had who cared for me, I had no one else to turn to at this moment in time, to think no one else cared or would ask whether I was dead or alive, it was a sad reality and it really brought it home bringing it back up in court. I knew at the end of the day this was an application for a visit visa so the reason for refusal by the Embassy was due to their belief that Ali wouldn't return and would become an over stayer, which almost demonstrated that they believed our relationship was so genuine that they had concerns Ali would abuse the visit visa. I reassured the judge telling him our plan was eventually to apply for a spouse visa when I turned 21, so why would we jeopardise this by Ali overstaying and tarnishing his home office record or any chance he would have. I was essentially having to wait 2 yrs to start a life with my husband due to a change in the UK law regarding the spouse visa, it was unfair and affecting us adversely. Surely, he could at least visit me for a period so we could have some sort of reasonable relations and contact as husband and wife.

The judge seemed impressed with our testimony and Nazreen's piece, he didn't say much but his silence was somewhat reassuring, he seemed interested and ready to listen, he told us we would get his decision soon in writing.

As we left court Zahira took me shopping to the local Asian area in Birmingham to take my mind off things. I tried to act interested and appreciated her efforts but I kept re playing what happened in the court room over and over again. This was my one chance, what if it went wrong? Did I say enough? I didn't know how I was to wait patiently or the decision but we had to prepare ourselves either way. We bought a few bits from an Islamic superstore for her own Islamic shop in Northampton and a few hijabs for her daughters and had a bite to eat. It was a Friday and I looked forward to going home to lay my head down for the weekend in anticipation of what was about to come.

The Visit

The following Monday was a bank holiday, I noticed a plain white envelope in the post which I didn't think much of. I walked upstairs to my room and started to casually open it, as I did I realised it looked official. My heart started pounding, but it couldn't be the decision from the Judge already, we had only been to court the Friday before. As I tore through it frantically, it read

NOTICE OF DECISION
Ali Khan Niazai VS The Home Office

I froze, this was what we had been waiting for, I tried to read through it calmly and understand it but I found myself trawling to the bottom to get to the decision which read 'the appeal is allowed'. I almost fainted, I read it repeatedly, at first I thought does that mean yes or no. What does the appeal is allowed mean, it's been allowed for the home office so refused for us? I became confused although I was 80% sure Ali was successful. So, I rang Nazreen to confirm and she congratulated us, 'you've both done a great job, if only all my clients were as prepared with their documents as you were, you truly both deserve it and I'm very happy for you. One quality Ali liked about me is my organisation, if I needed him to buy or do something I would leave a list for him with the relevant paperwork behind it to make it easier. When I used to visit Nazreen, she would comment on how well prepared all my documentation was and how others would simply walk into her office with a few papers in their hand hoping to submit an application. Having read up so much and having all this knowledge now on the immigration laws and rights of an individual she would joke that I should be doing her job and how I'd genuinely be great at it.

Having confirmed with Nazreen I broke the news to Ali, he was ecstatic and couldn't believe it. I wanted to joke with him as he always did with me and tell him it was refused first then break it to him but I couldn't do it, I was too shocked and excited. I felt pleased to be able to give him this good news and heard the hope in his voice as he was bored and lonely being away from me with nothing much to do. I couldn't stop thinking we had gone to court on, Friday, following which was a weekend then bank holiday Monday which meant the judge must have written his decision the same day as it had the court stamp on it dated the bank holiday. This is un heard of, surely judges or courts for that matter don't work on bank holidays?

God works in mysterious ways, it made me think more about our fate and this was just one of those things, another sign. I prayed that night thanking Allah for giving us the strength to get through this, I knew the journey wasn't over but I was so grateful. Allah tests the ones he loves or the ones he wants to bring closer to him and I certainly felt closer to my faith.

Ali shared the news with his family who were over the moon for us, they couldn't bear seeing us apart and constantly prayed for us to be together again soon. Ali quickly travelled to Pakistan to pick up his visa so he could book his ticket and travel to the UK however the embassy started messing him around saying the UK need to provide some confirmation before they issue it. It was all a load of rubbish and the longer they made him wait, he was losing days off his 6 month visit visa already issued and waiting. Nazreen tried to help and I even contacted our local MP but it didn't work, these people were disgusting. After everything we had been through and they still didn't want to release the visa, call it jealousy, envy, anger, I was annoyed beyond belief. Ali ended up paying someone to get it issued swiftly without the need for anything further to be provided, that's one of the things I learned throughout the process, unfortunately bribery gets you a long way in those countries.

Ali finally booked his ticket for a few days' time and did a little bit of shopping whilst also saying his goodbyes to his family in Afghanistan and cousins in Pakistan. He would be flying directly from Islamabad to London Heathrow and I couldn't wait! I counted the days down and couldn't sleep with excitement. I thought about that moment I would meet him at the airport but I didn't want to be disappointed, I had already learnt in life anything could happen, we continued to chat about our plans for when he would come over, we were just both so grateful for this opportunity.

The day finally came when Ali was flying over, I was beyond excited as I hadn't seen him in months but part of me was still dreading that I would have to let him go again, I told myself I would think about the here and now and deal with the goodbyes when the time came. I bought a banner, flowers and balloons to decorate our room to welcome him and cooked a few of his favourite dishes. The landlord Gurdip would come back and forth to collect rent and sometimes he would stop to chat and catch up with me, he was genuinely interested in our situation and wellbeing. I let him know that Ali was coming back and I knew the rent would increase again slightly to allow for a second person but that was fine.

I got to the airport on the coach, it was the cheapest way direct from our house as the train station was a fair walk but the bus station was down the road. Whilst I tried to find the arrivals gate I saw a young guy running a charity raffle for machinery at a local hospital for sick children and it looked like the prize was a big teddy bear. I would usually avoid these things at first glance but I was so happy about Ali coming home that I approached the guy and paid some money for the raffle, it was my good deed, a token of thanks for the good news we had just had I told myself. The guy was Asian, either Pakistani or Bengali, he thanked me for my contribution and noted my phone number on the back of the raffle ticket as they would draw the winner very soon. I walked off without giving it another thought, about an hour later I had a call from a number I didn't recognise. I thought it could be Ali so I picked up, to my surprise it was someone else, another man.

'Hi, is this Afia' he said,

'Yes' I answered hesitating.

'It's me the guy from the charity raffle, I hope you don't mind but I got your number from the raffle ticket.

'Urrrm ok' I answered, I knew where this was going. 'I'm actually here to pick up my husband who I'm very happy to see after a long time' I answered,

'Oh no I'm so sorry, he said. I'm so sorry to bother you, I didn't know, I'll get rid of your number'

'Ok' I replied 'just be careful next time'. I wasn't angry, I was too excited about Ali coming to be angry but part of me was annoyed that he used the contact details provided specifically for the raffle although I knew he meant no harm.

Ali took a while to come out, longer than expected as there was a lot of questioning at the airport considering where he was coming from and to ensure the validity of the passport/visa. Eventually he appeared, I looked at him from afar, he looked so different but the same? A sense of relief came over me as I started to walk towards him and embrace him with a big hug, I could see slight embarrassment on his face at the public affection but I didn't care.

I had been taking driving lessons but hadn't passed a test yet as I was too pre-occupied with everything else so we got a coach home and chatted the whole way. We were just so grateful to finally be with each other in person for a while, like a normal married couple. The 6 month visit flew by as you would expect, we bought a car that Ali drove, just a little run around to get us about and use for the time being. I worked and supported us both while we just enjoyed the time we had together. I felt somewhat strong and empowered, like we could do anything together, we visited Nazreen with gifts to personally thank her, not just as a solicitor but as a caring human being, like auntie Nazreen. When I would visit her about the case, she would try to re assure me, 'I see cases like this all the time, your situation is genuine don't worry just leave it to Allah' she would say. She knew I was stressing out and used to tell me to try to get some rest, take a relaxing bath with oils and candles she'd say and other times she'd comment on me looking thin and tired as she knew me well by now.

Ali spent time re connecting with his friends and we attended our first wedding together as a married couple. It was my Senior Advisor from my team Debbie's wedding which took place at a beautiful local venue, it was good to attend something together and different for us as this was our first English wedding ceremony invite. When I was alone, I tried to socialise but I just felt lonely and started to distance myself from people, I was in my own bubble but now I had Ali beside me. It was such a nice feeling to spend time together doing everyday things like food shopping, seeing friends or going for a meal. I managed to envy people who could do these things whenever they wanted, if only they appreciated how good they have it I thought.

The room we were renting from Gurdip, at Margaret Street was literally a street away from dad's other restaurant. A few doors down from the restaurant was a halal butchers ran by a Bangladeshi family. Back in the day we would go there with dad often after doing a home and restaurant food shop. He would take us to the restaurant to help un pack, when we had finished he would ask us what we wanted to eat and make us fresh poppadum's and kebabs as a treat. Sometimes he'd take us to the butchers whilst he placed orders, the guy at the till would give us sweets and crisps whenever he saw us. Today this was our local halal butchers, I had no choice but to go there as without a car at least I could easily carry what I had bought home. At first, I didn't think the guy recognised me but the more often I would go the more intrigued he became. Whilst Ali was around we would go together and eventually he approached us. He told us he remembered me and of course still knew and was friends with my dad, on one visit we talked at length. He said he had heard about what had happened and whilst he didn't comment on the circumstances, there was something he said that surprised me. Although I couldn't care less what anyone had to say about what we had done let alone the local community, he said 'I know you have seen some tough days and I know your dad is a very proud man but now I have met you both and see your intentions I'm sure it is a matter of time before your dad understands this and accepts you both'. I recognise this man didn't have to say this and when he said it, it was very heart felt, I could see him almost welling up. He went on to give Ali his business card with the phone number of the shop, 'if she needs any help or wants us to bring over something from the shop if she can't get to us then just ring' he said, 'it's not a problem'. This stuck with us both and meant so much, he was one of the first people in the Bengali community to openly accept our situation, who wasn't afraid to say it and genuinely offered us some support.

Our time together quickly drew to a close, we made some memories and the visit gave us hope. We had to prepare ourselves to be separated all over again but this time we knew what to expect and were so grateful for the time we had just spent together, essentially our first time living together alone as a married couple. On 29th April 10 we got the train to the airport as I decided to drop Ali off, I don't know why but I suppose it meant we could spend a few last moments together. I waited for him to check in and walked him up as far as I could, we said our goodbyes and both walked off. I didn't look back as tears began to flow, I didn't want him to see me break down, I got back on the coach to go home alone in a daze staring out the window.

Ali got back home to Afghan safely, we got his family a few gifts to take back but they were just so happy that he could spend some time with me and lead somewhat of a normal life. It was now just more waiting for me to turn 21 as Ali couldn't come again on another visit as there had to be at least a 6 month gap in between the last family visit. Whilst we were waiting Ali got himself a job in the Afghan army to keep him occupied. He became a translator for the American troops working for the Afghan Army, he worked very close to his home, Bagram Airbase, you can literally see the base from the roof of his house. The Americans couldn't get enough of his British accent and how fluently he could speak English in comparison to other translators. Although the application process was long and tough going through written & physical tests before being thoroughly screened, he made good friends with the troops. He got on well with his Major, Major Matthews who looked after him and really respected him. They would constantly crack jokes on duty and Ali would be his first choice of translator when they needed to question any of the locals, detainees or visitors. Major Matthews has a family back in America whom he would visit when he was on leave, he would treat Ali well and regularly offer him the key to the Army pantry, take anything you want anytime he would say as he trusted him like a brother.

Ali would wear his uniform and heavy body armour whilst on patrol, some days we wouldn't get to speak on the phone because of the timings of his shifts but I didn't mind. I was relieved he had something to keep him busy and make a little spending money for himself otherwise he would have been crawling the walls. He was working at the base a few months, it was now the new year which meant my holiday allowance at work had been refreshed. I could now come out to visit and bring all the paperwork with me for the upcoming spouse visa application we were planning to submit. I was busy preparing the reams of phone calls, payslips, bank statements, wedding photos, letters from friends and anything else that would help. We were both dreading the prospect of being refused again and going through the appeals process, whilst there was no reason to be refused we knew by now that anything could happen.

The Finish Line

Whilst Ali was working with the army I carried on at the bank, just keeping my head down and getting on with it. By this time my team were like my family and knew about everything that was going on, they fully supported me and tried to help whenever they could. Debbie continued to mother me, offering me lifts for shopping and just in general, I went around to her house for dinner one night and just chilled. She had gone out of her way to buy halal meat and cook me dinner, the love that she showed me is something special and I truly respect her for that. She ferried me to and from the airport a few times, taking me for a meal before to calm me down and just generally filling in as a mother as best she could. Although like anyone she had things going on in her own life she always made time for me. She was my rock, my shoulder to cry on the days when it all got too much and the one who had faith in my strength and ability. She would often say, 'Af I may not 100% understand your culture or religion but I really respect and am so proud of you for what you have gone through and what you are doing as a young, independent woman and wife'.

Whilst working at the bank I met another girl from another department, Farhana. She was an advisor on the phone and I had seen her around a few times assuming she was Pakistani from her appearance. However, I came to know she was Bengali and had a similar back story to mine although she had a small family of her own whom she was living with happily. We got to know each other and became good friends, she would pick me up and take me round her house to chill out as she lived local, she would call me every now and again to make sure I was ok and not just sitting around stressing out. She knew my situation and I suppose she could relate, I often felt embarrassed and annoyed that I couldn't invite her to my place as I still lived in a room in a house which was not appropriate for guests. She tried to include me in anything she could and I often spent Ramadan and Eid at her place which is usually quite a family time so she knew I would be thinking of them. I would in turn babysit for her and her husband to give them a break, I enjoyed it and grew to love her kids but also felt I was able to give something back, she introduced me to some of her friends and really looked after me.

The days and months seemed to drag on and I became depressed about the whole situation, I would think so deeply about being so far away from my husband due to the distance between us and the law that separated us. When I was feeling down I had this strange feeling of guilt, not wanting to eat hot meals, the thought of having a home cooked hot meal made me feel sick. My mentality was that home cooked meals are for happy families to enjoy, I didn't feel like I deserved or that I had earnt it. I couldn't even do one thing right to bring my husband into the country so why should I have the luxury of a hot meal?, also what was the point of cooking a nice meal for me to enjoy alone? I would often have sandwiches for dinner or if I had something hot it was pasta. I stopped going to the butchers and stopped eating meat, instead I would have Quorn mince every now and again. I never felt like having a takeaway, it was like everything nice and enjoyable should be enjoyed with someone, who sits in on their own and has a takeaway anyway I thought. I just wanted to sit in my room and be left alone, some days I would literally not say a word as I was on my own if I didn't contact anyone I didn't have to say anything. I began to lose weight and become drained, loss of weight through stress is not a healthy loss but rather it just made my face and bones stick out. People would comment on my appearance in a concerned tone but they didn't know what I was going through, I wasn't ill, I'm just one of those people who doesn't eat when I'm upset.

On the way home from work one day I came off the bus into the bus station, my normal stop and headed towards Sainsburys. This was my closest supermarket in walking distance, when I got there I had to buy a few food bits and some washing powder. I looked at the washing powder and realised if I went for a bigger box it would be better value but then I thought if I buy a bigger box then I can't buy anything else today as I won't be able to carry it all home, so I had to make a choice. These were the little things in my life that reminded me of my situation, Ali would often tell me to get a taxi home if I had a lot of shopping but I would rather spend the taxi fare on credit ringing him.

I managed to visit Ali once more within the year when my holiday allowance renewed at work, I looked forward to that 3 weeks so much and cherished the time we shared together. By now his family were besotted with me and treated me like royalty, they always worried about me and what I was used to or didn't have. This time when I came I travelled through Pakistan, Ali would drop me off back to Pakistan for my flight and we decided to spend a couple of days there in Islamabad. We stayed with his cousins in their house, they were very hospitable and a big family of quite a few girls. They loved me coming and made every effort with me, they were skilled at applying henna so as soon as I would enter they would sit me down and start henna on my hands whilst another would braid my hair. We visited some beautiful places with them whilst we were there and took plenty of photos for memories and to use for our upcoming visa submission. I would laugh at myself sometimes, born and bred in Northampton but when I was away from the UK I felt loved and like one of their own somewhere so many miles away.

I'm not going to lie and say it got easier because it didn't and that's just life sometimes, the other tenants in the house changed all the time as you can imagine in any rented accommodation. There was this woman in the attic room with her creepy uncle whom I used to try to avoid when I knew he was around. I just wouldn't come out of my room, one night I was so hungry and wanted to make dinner but I knew he was here in the kitchen so I just had some crisps for dinner instead which may sound quite extreme but that is how uncomfortable he would make you feel. The way he would check you out up and down and he was my dad's age, it made me feel sick and I would wrap up head to toe whenever he was around

Then there was a guy downstairs who was lovely but one day he had an argument with two other girls in the house and started punching the kitchen door which scared the hell out of everyone. Then there was another girl who almost treated her room like a brothel and asked to use my WIFI a few times which I didn't mind but it got to a point where she would knock on my door at 7am on a sat morning for the Wi-Fi access which would really annoy me of course. There were others who stayed who were genuinely nice, normal, friendly people but the majority were wild which made it scary for me as a young girl living on my own. One afternoon I was in my room and forgot to lock the door after I came from the bathroom, I was only watching tv but someone burst into my room, it was a friend of the tenant in the next room who thought my room was the bathroom.

I even got stalked when I was in Sainsburys a few times by the same guy just trying to get my attention, it's a scary world all on your own and it didn't suit me.

These are the kind of things I had to deal with daily, for a young girl from an Asian background who's been somewhat sheltered her whole life it was the unknown to me and I had to grow a pair to survive.

The time finally came around for me to fly out to Afghan just before my 21st birthday which would be when we could officially submit our new application. Before I left I went to see Nazreen for her to have a look over all the documents and application and ensure nothing was missing. Again, it was the reams of call records, photos, marriage certificate, references from friends, payslips, bank statements and anything else I could find to help convince the investigating officer that this was a genuine, happy marriage. If anything, we knew that their refusal of the previous 6 month family visit visa strengthened this case as at that time their reason for refusal was that they didn't think Ali would return, so by default they had given the impression that they had no doubts around our relationship at that time but I still knew it couldn't be that simple.

I spent time with the family whilst I was there, this time in April so it was spring season in Afghan. It was exciting knowing it might be the last time I travelled there to see him in these circumstances and hopefully next time we could both go together. I stayed for 3 weeks and caught up with everyone, when I left, Ali once again made the trip to Pakistan to submit his visa application. He attended the appointment to submit, paid the now increased fee and we continued to wait on tenterhooks for the decision. This was what we had been waiting for, all those years of hard work and waiting around, our lives were essentially in someone else's hands. I knew we always had the option to appeal but why should we, what could go wrong this time, I couldn't bear thinking about it.

Within 6-8 weeks we received the news we had been waiting for, they rang Ali and asked him to come in to collect the decision as they couldn't tell him over the phone. He rang me at work with the news, tears of joy and relief came gushing down my face as I couldn't believe it, they had granted him the spouse visa first time, without any fight, it was finally over, the nightmare had ended.

'I couldn't have done this without you Jaan' he proclaimed proudly, 'we have both worked hard but I won't forget what you have given up. Thank you for being our strength and everything you have done for us, now we can spend the rest of our lives together inshallah'.

Present Day … 22 July 2018

What we have been through has made us incredibly stronger and an experience I would not change or forget. It was a very difficult time in our lives that taught us both so much in relation to loyal friends/family and how to mature into adults fast when the situation calls for it. I truly believe that God chose for us to be together no matter what, we just had to work hard to ensure that the path of fate didn't change.

Today we have our health, a home, friends, wealth and a good happy relationship with both sides of the family. It took a while for my dad to come around but in the end, he knew his daughter's happiness was key and the fact that we are together today stronger than ever, broke his theories of doubt.

Don't ever give up on something worth fighting for, something you really believe in, something you desire. If it's meant to be, it will come to you, there's no need to chase it and if not, then there is something better coming your way.

This novel marks our 10 year wedding anniversary of 22nd July 2018 and whilst we may have changed in appearance, we are still the same Ali & Afia who took a chance on love with a pure, clean heart and every strength we could find.

When I am asked why I made those choices, why I decided to leave everything I knew, my safe place of 16 years for someone you could say I barely knew at the time? With a smile I reply, because I believed in us, in our love, in our story.

Always be humble, be grateful & never forget your past, your beginning, your journey.

Shukr Alhamdulilah- All praise be to God.

Treasures to remember

A cross stitch pattern I completed over a few months whilst I was living alone in the rented room waiting for Home Office decisions. This would calm me down when I was stressed or upset and give me something to focus my anger & energies on.

Today it brings a smile to my face as it hangs framed in our bedroom, pride of place.

When Ali came over on the six month visit we went for a short break to Bournemouth, our favourite beach. It was something a 'normal' couple without craziness in their lives could do and we felt invincible, finally back together, ready to take on the world.

On the way home from London after getting my Afghan visa before Ali was to leave for good he bought me roses from the random people on the street, that you see in the middle of the road or even roundabout.

It was very unexpected and whilst I loved the gesture it made me emotional thinking of the goodbyes when he presented them to me.

The sixth month visit visa appeal document, this was make or break for us and still makes me nervous when I see an official immigration document.

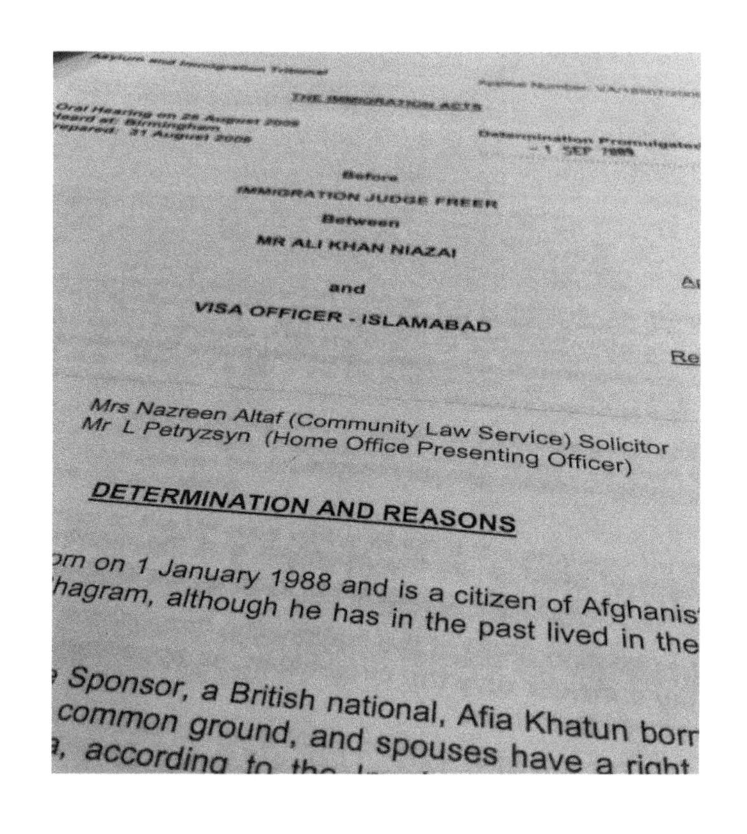

Asylum and Immigration Tribunal

THE IMMIGRATION ACTS

Heard at: Birmingham

Determination Promulgated

Before

IMMIGRATION JUDGE FREER

Between

MR ALI KHAN NIAZAI

and

VISA OFFICER - ISLAMABAD

Mrs Nazreen Altaf (Community Law Service) Solicitor
Mr L Petryzsyn (Home Office Presenting Officer)

DETERMINATION AND REASONS

...orn on 1 January 1988 and is a citizen of Afghanis...
...hagram, although he has in the past lived in the...

...Sponsor, a British national, Afia Khatun born...
...common ground, and spouses have a right...
...according to the...

The final decision page of the appeal document from the judge with his summary.

I respect his words and the advice he gave us, it evidences genuine care & concern.

The fact it was dated on a bank holiday, just gives me the chills thinking this was fate. This judge has no idea how much this meant to us, it literally gave us so much happiness and kept us going for the long term.

Judge Freer, thank you for giving a husband & wife hope and a chance to make some priceless memories.

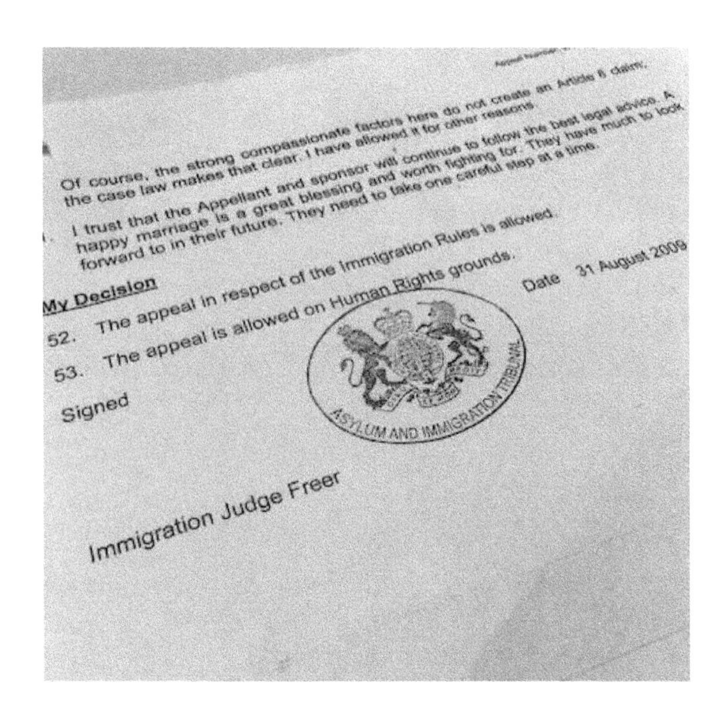

Of course, the strong compassionate factors here do not create an Article 8 claim; the case law makes that clear. I have allowed it for other reasons

I trust that the Appellant and sponsor will continue to follow the best legal advice. A happy marriage is a great blessing and worth fighting for. They have much to look forward to in their future. They need to take one careful step at a time.

My Decision

52. The appeal in respect of the Immigration Rules is allowed.

53. The appeal is allowed on Human Rights grounds.

Signed Date 31 August 2009

ASYLUM AND IMMIGRATION TRIBUNAL

Immigration Judge Freer

Summary from the appeal document when the judge praised Nazreen Altaaf our solicitor, it supports why we truly believe she is one in a million & went above and beyond.

Nazreen you are truly amazing!

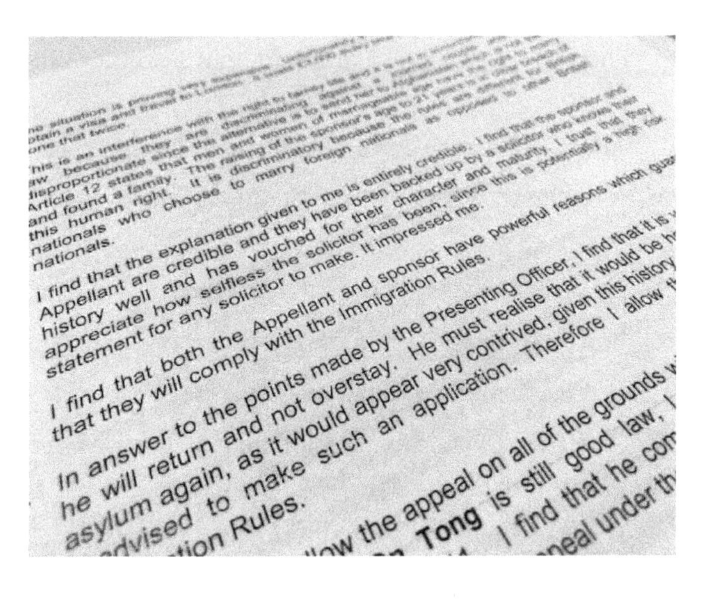

I find that the explanation given to me is entirely credible. I find that the sponsor and Appellant are credible and they have been backed up by a solicitor who knows their history well and has vouched for their character and maturity. I trust that they appreciate how selfless the solicitor has been, since this is potentially a high risk statement for any solicitor to make. It impressed me.

I find that both the Appellant and sponsor have powerful reasons which gua
that they will comply with the Immigration Rules.

In answer to the points made by the Presenting Officer, I find that it is
he will return and not overstay. He must realise that it would be h
asylum again, as it would appear very contrived, given this history
advised to make such an application. Therefore I allow th
tion Rules.

llow the appeal on all of the grounds
Tong is still good law,
I find that he com
peal under th

They said we wouldn't make it

They said it wouldn't work

They said we were too different, that he'd turn out to be a jerk.

They said it wasn't worth it, that we shouldn't try.

That he wouldn't love me but instead he'd make me cry

They told me I would regret

They warned me to stay away

But it was only him that made me smile each day

They tried to change my mind, tell me it wasn't yet my time

And for minute I started to listen……………..

People said he wasn't cultured

People said we should forget

But Allah had other plans for us which is why we met

We saw tough times ahead, no food, home, or cash

But no matter what I always had for you love, a big stash!

Alhamdulillah, we made it Jaan, we fought, we survived, we won.

The story has only just begun, inshallah we are going to have much more fun.

For we are a gift for each other from God, the almighty, the all-knowing, the one

People talked, gossiped, warned but where did they go?

Who were they? Friend or foe?

Q. re family } - Was Afia concerned about what they "could" do?

Q - current situation in Afghanistan.

Q - What would you tell your 16 yr old self now

Q -

Lightning Source UK Ltd.
Milton Keynes UK
UKHW020638300721
388036UK00014B/1501